Thames
in the Country

David Sharp is a Vice President of the Ramblers. Having masterminded the Ramblers' first survey of a potential route along the Thames, he then led the campaign to gain its recognition, especially as author of the bestselling Ramblers' guide to the walk. With his wife Margaret, he has explored the river for over 40 years, watching the Thames Path gradually take shape.

Tony Gowers is a freelance writer and countryside access consultant who lives in the picturesque village of Wye in Kent. He has a passion for walking and has completed many National Trails and other long-distance routes. Until recently he was the National Trail Officer for the North Downs Way.

Thames Path
in the Country

David Sharp
and Tony Gowers

Aurum

in association with

NATURAL
ENGLAND

Acknowledgements

On behalf of all who enjoy the Thames Path, now or in the future, I would like to record my thanks to those who made it possible. To Leigh Hatts for proving that it was feasible; to Jenny Blair for drawing it all together in a massive report; and to Jane Bowden, Simon Fisher, Maggie Grenham and Karin Groeneveld for all their efforts in turning it into reality.   DS

I would like to thank Jos Joslin, National Trails Manager for the Thames Path, for all her knowledge, help and enthusiasm towards updating this volume. I would also like to thank my partner Val for putting up with me while I have been researching, walking, etc., etc!   TG

Published in 2012 by Aurum Press Ltd
7 Greenland Street, London NW1 0ND
in association with Natural England.
www.naturalengland.org.uk
www.nationaltrail.co.uk
First published in an earlier form in 2003 as *The Thames Path* by David Sharp

Text copyright © 2012 by Aurum Press Ltd and Natural England

Pictures are copyright © the photographer/agency and are by: 8–9, 18–19, 23, 24, 30, 32, 43, 57, 67, 71, 78, 79, 117, 125, 127, 131, 134, 145 and 149 Tony Gowers; 45, 75 and 97 David Sharp; 10, 11, 15, 36, 39, 61, 107, 120, 122, 136 and 150 Rob Fraser/Natural England; 26–7 River Thames Alliance; 51 and 138 Anne-Katrin Purkiss/Natural England; 82–3 Jos Joslin; 2–3, 13, 14 (top and middle), 16 (both), 20 (top and middle), 29, 47, 56, 59, 62, 69, 94, 104–5, 108–9, 113, 115, 143, 152 and 157 Alamy; 14 (bottom) © The Estate of Stanley Spencer 2012, all rights reserved, DACS/The Bridgeman Art Library); 21 © Dulwich Picture Gallery, London, UK /The Bridgeman Art Library; 89 The Bridgeman Art Library; 111 Geoffrey Swaine/Rex Features; 53 Flickr; 129 Corbis; 20 (bottom) RIBA Library Drawings & Archives Collections; 130 Getty Images; 132 Tate, London 2012.

OS Ordnance Survey® This product includes mapping data licensed from Ordnance Survey® with the permission of the Controller of Her Majesty's Stationery Office. © Crown copyright 2012. All rights reserved. Licence number 43453U.

Ordnance Survey, Pathfinder and Travelmaster are registered trademarks and the Ordnance Survey symbol and Explorer are trademarks of Ordnance Survey, the national mapping agency of Great Britain.

A catalogue record for this book is available from the British Library.

ISBN 978 1 84513 717 5

Book design by Robert Updegraff
Printed and bound in China

Cover photograph: *The Thames at Windsor (right bank) and Eton (left bank): The Image Bank/Getty Images*
Half-title page: *The Roundhouse, upstream of Lechlade (Anne-Katrin Purkiss/Natural England)*
Title page: *The Thames at Stanton Harcourt (Alamy)*

Aurum Press want to ensure that these National Trail Guides are always as up to date as possible – but stiles collapse, pubs close and bus services change all the time. If, on walking this path, you discover any important changes of which future walkers need to be aware, do let us know. Either email us on **trailguides@aurumpress.co.uk** with your comments, or if you take the trouble to drop us a line to:

Trail Guides, Aurum Press, 7 Greenland Street, London NW1 0ND,
we'll send you a free guide of your choice as thanks.

Contents

Key map

the Thames Path

1 chapter start point

0 km   10
0 miles   10

How to use this guide

This guide is divided into three sections:

Introduction

This includes an introduction to the Thames Path and to the river itself, including history, flora and fauna, locks and weirs, bridges and islands. It also includes practical advice on walking the route and a list of other long-distance paths which intersect with the country section of the Thames Path.

Thames Path in the Country

The route is described in 12 sections. At the start of each its distance in miles and kilometres is given, together with an overview of that stretch of the path and information on public transport links. The names of 'things to look out for' are shown

in bold blue type, together with a reference number also shown on the maps. The main part of each section consists of the actual route description, accompanied by the relevant map with the route marked in yellow. Also appearing in the text and on the maps are reference letters to help with route-finding and symbols as shown in the inside front cover of this book. Arrows (➜) at the edge of the maps indicate the start point. Each section ends with information on transport, refreshments and accommodation.

Useful information

Contact details for public transport, accommodation, tourist information and other organisations.

Distance checklist

location	approx. distance from previous location	
	miles	km
The Source	–	–
Ashton Keynes	7.0	11.2
Cricklade	5.3	8.5
Castle Eaton	4.3	6.9
Lechlade	6.7	10.8
Radcot	6.3	10.0
Newbridge	10.0	16.0
Swinford	7.8	12.6
Oxford	6.2	9.9
Abingdon	9.7	15.6
Culham	2.2	3.5
Wallingford	11.3	18.2
Cholsey	3.2	5.2
Goring	3.9	6.3
Pangbourne	4.2	6.8
Tilehurst	3.5	5.6
Reading	3.4	5.5
Shiplake	6.7	10.7
Henley	2.2	3.5
Marlow	8.5	13.7
Maidenhead	7.6	12.2
Windsor	6.7	10.8
Staines	8.3	13.3
Shepperton	5.5	8.8
Hampton Court	6.2	10.0

Introduction

This book describes the first 147 miles (235 km) of the Thames Path National Trail, from its source deep in the Cotswolds as far as Hampton Court on the outskirts of London. The remainder of the Thames Path is now covered in a new Aurum Press volume, *Thames Path in London*, which describes the route from Hampton Court through Central London to the Thames Barrier and continues on the Thames Path Extension.

A great river walk

It may not always be where you expect it, but at one spring or another in the gentle folds of Cotswold meadow around Ewen you will meet the first trickles of moving water and know that you have found the birthplace of the Thames. At the other end of your 147-mile (235-km) journey, you will see that same water as a vast river approaching London. Between the two, you will experience a living river, from gentle birth, through the artless freedom of youth, to the proud symbols of maturity – the castles and colleges, churches and royal palaces that line its banks. All rivers can be rewarding to explore, but the Thames is something special, one of the world's great rivers, flowing serenely through the pages of our history.

For many years, such a journey was more dream than reality, but the launch of the Thames Path in 1996 opened it up to join our other National Trails. As a walking experience it is distinctly different from the rest of the National Trails. First, because it is a very easy walk, as accessible to the stroller as to the die-hard long-distance walker. It offers no rugged hill climbs or vast moorland expanses by way of challenge; indeed the Thames never seems to be going anywhere in a hurry, and the mood is catching. The good public transport facilities along the Thames Valley help, as they make it temptingly easy to plan short walks. Many people explore the Thames in this way, taking it in easy stages – covering a single section on one day and then returning a few weeks later to carry on where they left off. Thus you can walk the Thames Path in two weeks, two years, or a lifetime. Old Father Thames seems to encourage this leisurely approach, always there to welcome you back and see you off on the next stage.

The second difference is in the remarkable variety it offers, a progression of experience from the lonely, open watermeadows of its headwaters to the bustling anticipation of a great city. Even a single day's walk can offer this variety, as the Thames Path takes you from the busy waterside of a little township – Henley perhaps – around a bend or two into river scenes of total tranquillity, where a heron will flap away in surprise that anyone has intruded into its solitude.

History of the Thames Path

The creation of a long walk by the Thames is no new idea. Even in the early 1930s, local authorities along the river were getting together to discuss how the old Thames towing path could be put to new use. It was no longer needed for its original purpose, yet it was there, following the river from Putney, deep in London, up to Lechlade on the edge of the Cotswolds. The Thames Commissioners were responsible for establishing the towpath back in the late 18th century, at a time when the river was beginning to play an essential role in the burgeoning canal system. It proved a difficult task, as the Thames is no canal but a living river, and every so often the towpath met obstacles, natural or man-made, and got around them by changing to the opposite bank. At these problem points, a navigation ferry had to be provided to carry the towing teams across. A mile above Lechlade, the towpath left the Thames entirely to follow a new navigation, the Thames and Severn Canal.

Visionary though they were, those 1930s debates could do little to create a long-distance walk, and it was not until 1949 that Parliament provided the means of doing this, on a national scale. Not surprisingly, the embryonic idea of re-using the Thames towpath came top of the list of routes for consideration. But, ironically, this proved to be the worst possible time for considering a walk along the river. The navigation ferries, so vital to the continuity of the towpath, were no longer economical and were closing down. Other routes were clearly easier to create, and the Thames idea was put to one side, all too likely to be forgotten.

Two bodies were determined that this should not happen – the River Thames Society and the Ramblers' Association. They worked together, and in 1977 the Ramblers published a new concept for a walk that would require no ferries. Moreover, it enlarged on the original idea of a towpath walk by carrying it on via little-used paths to discover the source itself, in that faraway Gloucestershire meadow.

It revived interest to a point where, in 1984, the Countryside Commission (now Natural England) published the results of a study that declared the concept to be feasible, the likely costs reasonable and the recreational value high. The route was officially declared a National Trail in

Rural serenity – remote Northmoor Lock is reflected in the still waters of the Thames.

1987 and, after a vast amount of work into improving its line and raising it to the highest standards, it opened in 1996. Three new footbridges provided much-needed river crossings, miles of new riverside footpaths were patiently negotiated with landowners and stiles were replaced by gates, combining to make the Thames Path more easily accessible.

The section through London and Docklands in particular, described fully in the accompanying National Trail Guide *The Thames Path in London*, still sees exciting developments. Once it seemed that the walk must end where the towpath ends, at Putney Bridge, but now you can keep on along either bank, often on walkways created as features of new riverside developments. Of course there are still a few points where you have, briefly, to leave the river. Perhaps a stubborn warehouse blocks the way, a site where the cranes and the hard hats are still working away, or even a fragment of surviving riverside industry. But today's Thames Path gives you a breathtaking new view of a great city – the view from the river. And even the few rough passages have something to say about the fabric of London, interludes before the next vast river scene opens up. And there could be no more powerful image with which to end the complete Thames Path walk than the mighty engineering triumph of the Thames Barrier.

Infant Thames

All the Cotswold rivers – Churn, Coln, Leach, Windrush, Evenlode and lesser names – flow down to add their waters to the Thames. There have been disputes as to the true source of the Thames, but the river we follow from Trewsbury Mead through the Keynes villages has for centuries been called Thames, and locals have never known it by any other name. This must be because it has always unquestionably been the main stream, and indeed barges once traded up to wharves at Waterhay Bridge.

So in the meadows above the hamlet of Ewen, the source springs of the Thames are all around you, though only rarely, in very wet seasons, will you see water at the highest spring marked by the stone where our Thames Path begins. Just above it ran the summit level of the Thames and Severn Canal, now dry, and through the years when a steam pump was raising water to it, this was naturally blamed for the absence of water in the valley springs. Now it is evident that the water table is lower than it once was. A Victorian visitor records walking hereabouts and producing fountains of water just by thrusting his stick into the grassy hillocks. It wouldn't happen today. But the water is down there still, and it would be fair to say that the true source of the Thames is beneath your feet. The lush valley slopes down to Ewen at a considerable angle, as do the water-bearing strata below, and from one spring or another water will burst to the surface. Walking down the valley, you will

A simple stone beneath an old ash tree marks the river's source.

...oot Bridge on the lonely upper reaches of the Thames.

pass several springs, the first in the bowl of meadow just beyond the Foss Way, which can be transformed into a lake after a rainy spell – and probably has the best claim to be the source. In another half mile you walk above Lyd Well, reputedly a Roman well and often flowing vigorously in its boggy enclosure. In Ewen itself, across the lane behind the Wild Duck Inn, you can look over the fence to a pool in a deep, tree-circled hollow – Monks' Pond, another spring which reliably feeds the Thames. Ewen comes from the Saxon *Æwylme*, meaning source of a river – and that says it all.

Lonely Thames

As it flows through Cricklade to Lechlade the Thames grows from modest stream to lovely young river, broad and confident enough to carry the big white cruisers that gather at the head of navigation. Then from St John's Lock down to Oxford it takes on a quality of loneliness, meandering through its wide, flat flood plain of Oxford clay. Beware those loops; they can make your walk far longer than it appears from a glance at the map. No villages, no farmsteads come near the river, the only human habitation is the occasional lock cottage or isolated inn. With no sound of road or rattle of railway, to some this is a stretch of blissful escape. A string of communities, like the market town of Bampton, and villages such as Aston, Longworth, Buckland, Appleton and Northmoor, would consider themselves to be 'by the Thames', but they keep to the gravel terraces a mile or two back from the river.

The routes to the river crossings have always been important here, leading first to fords, then trackways down to the early bridges. Thus the town of Faringdon once had a castle standing guard over the ancient packhorse crossing at Radcot. At times of unrest, the crossings were fought over. Radcot Bridge saw the Earl of Oxford's defeat by Henry Bolingbroke's forces in 1387, then became a Royalist outpost in the Civil War, when its final capture by Fairfax forced King Charles to abandon Oxford. Newbridge, too, saw bitter Civil War encounters, but it is difficult today to associate these peaceful spots with the clash of arms. This is a Thames of far-stretching watermeadows under a vast, open arc of sky, bringing an odd 'top of the world' feeling as you walk for miles with just a herd or two of inquisitive young cattle for company. Past travellers made constant reference to the elms, and their stately presence must have added a grander dimension to the landscape. The elms were lost in the 1970s, but still it is the trees that define and punctuate these river scenes, taking the Thames Path through ever-changing compositions that are the very essence of English countryside.

Early Thames

From Oxford on, you are meeting the earliest valley settlements. Access was good and, especially as trade began to move along the river and along the downland line of the Icknield Way, prehistoric man made his home on the dry gravel by the Thames. For sure, New Stone Age people brought agriculture, evidenced by many finds around Abingdon, and the later Beaker Folk left numerous traces between Abingdon and Stanton Harcourt, including a fine collection of bronze weapons found in the Thames near Sandford Lock. But though we can learn much from finds and crop-marks, it is not until you reach the hill fort on the Sinodun Hills, and the great earthworks of the Dyke Hills below, that the work of prehistoric man becomes obvious. The major settlements seem either to have been based on defensive needs or on fords. Oxford itself grew as an island stronghold between Thames and Cherwell, while Iron Age, Roman and Saxon Dorchester all sheltered between Thames and Thame in the same way.

As trade increased, the ford settlements like Wallingford grew in importance – in Saxon times the town even had a royal mint. Abingdon rose to prosperity with the foundation of its abbey, which soon become one of the richest in the land. Indeed, the old town still clearly stands around the abbey gates. For long it out-shone its rival, Wallingford, but its fords were long and treacherous, and Wallingford had not only a ford but also a bridge by the time William the Conqueror came seeking a crossing for his army. The Cotswold merchants preferred to take their precious woolpacks over Wallingford Bridge rather than risk a ford, so the Abingdon merchants had to raise money to build both Abingdon and Culham

bridges and a long causeway between them. Thus, in 1422, they won their trade back. The bridges and the causeway still stand, and Wallingford has both Saxon ramparts and the battered traces of a castle demolished after falling to the Roundheads – visual reminders of how the early pages of our history unfolded along this stretch of the Thames.

Victorian Thames

Below Reading you are walking into the Thames of Victorian high summer, and at Henley you cannot escape reminders of its famous Royal Regatta, the spectacle the Victorians elevated to the very top of their social calendar. In the late 19th century everyone, from Cockney to society belle, flocked here, and in 1888 the peak day of the regatta brought 6,768 people along the little branch line to Henley. They saw the course lined by over 80 houseboats decked with colourful awnings, floral garlands and bunting. Fashionable crowds, the men in white flannels, striped blazers and straw hats, the ladies in their latest finery, spread across the river in punts, rowing boats and gondolas. Musicians entertained, picnic parties strolled the banks, and by evening light the lanterns and coloured globes of a Venetian carnival turned the river into fairyland. The rowing, of course, took second place!

Every Thames-side town from Oxford to Richmond had its regatta; indeed when Henley ended, the crowds would teem down to Marlow Regatta, which started the following day. And it was not just the regattas; the Victorians took passionately to boating along the river, either camping or putting up in riverside taverns. The Victorians, with their hampers and parasols, have departed but their spirit still haunts the middle Thames.

Royal Thames

As the Thames Path passes beneath Windsor Castle, you are reminded that you are following a royal river. Downstream a succession of palaces have stood by the water's edge, vying for royal favour from reign to reign. From the formalities of court and the foul air of London, our sovereigns escaped to their country estates, travelling by river with far more comfort and pageantry than by road. The gilded royal barge would be accompanied by musicians, courtiers and household in procession. The last state barge was retired after centuries to the Royal Maritime Museum, Greenwich, but the Queen's Bargemaster and Royal Watermen still attend state occasions in their finery.

Most monarchs since Henry II have favoured Windsor Castle, especially for its vast hunting forest, and today the Queen's standard often flies from the Round Tower. Victoria spent over £1 million on modernising her castle, and broke with tradition by travelling here by Royal Train. Cardinal Wolsey gave his vastly ostentatious palace of Hampton Court to Henry VIII in a vain bid to regain favour. Henry accepted it, and spent so much of his extravagant life there that two of his unfortunate wives still haunt it.

Literary Thames

The landscapes and scenic beauty of the River Thames have long inspired the most famous storytellers and poets of the day.

In Victorian times in particular there was a huge surge in popularity of all things to do with the river. Some wrote philosophically of their experiences, and Jerome K. Jerome, author of the classic

'The pipe of peace' – an illustration from Three Men in a Boat.

Three Men in a Boat, was only one of many who followed the vogue. His is probably the most famous tale of the Thames, describing a rowing adventure along the river to Pangbourne, with the author waxing lyrical about places he saw and stopped at along the way, including villages and watering holes. Today the Thames Path walker can visit the locations immortalised by Jerome, notably the Barley Mow at Clifton Hampden, The Bull at Sonning and The Swan at Pangbourne.

The Thames brought literary inspiration in other ways, too. When Charles Dodgson, a mathematics lecturer at Christ Church, Oxford, rowed three little girls to picnics at Godstow and Nuneham, he told them the fanciful stories that were published in 1865 as *Alice's Adventures in Wonderland* and in 1871 as *Through the Looking-Glass*. Kenneth Grahame lived much of his life by the river at Cookham and used his beloved stretch of river up to Pangbourne as a setting for the tales of Toad, Mole and Ratty, told first to his young son, then published as *The Wind in the Willows* in 1908. H. G. Wells was another famous writer who lived in Berkshire and loved the river, using some of his memories of it in his novel *The History of Mr Polly*.

Poets through the ages have immortalised the river and the places on its banks in their verse. The Elizabethan poet Edmund Spenser wrote 'Prothalamion' ('Wedding Song'), which includes the famous line 'Sweet Thames, run softly'. St Lawrence Church, Lechlade, overlooking the Thames, inspired Percy Bysshe Shelley in September 1815 to write 'A Summer Evening Churchyard', while William Morris wrote about his beloved Kelmscott (see page 56) in his poems 'Love Is Enough' and 'Earthly Paradise'. Matthew Arnold, the great 19th-century poet, who was born at Laleham on the Thames, wrote about the river in the *Scholar Gipsy* and described the ferry crossing point at Bablock Hythe. A poem by Rudyard Kipling, 'What Say the Reeds at Runnymede?', refers to the signing of the Magna Carta on the Thames, while in the 20th century John Betjeman's poems include 'Henley on Thames', and in *Summoned by Bells* he describes a boat trip up the river to Godstow.

Jerome K. Jerome

Matthew Arnold

Stanley Spencer

Artistic Thames

Artists have for many years been drawn to the Thames for the wonderful views and scenic landscapes along its course. Many have painted the river in central London, but the more rural parts of the Thames and the towns and villages on its banks have also been a source of inspiration.

Canaletto, the renowned Venetian artist, lived in London between 1746 and 1755 and painted Westminster Bridge. In 1754 he travelled upriver to Walton-on-Thames, capturing on canvas the intricate wooden bridge over the Thames in *Old Walton Bridge* (see Bridges, page 19).

Victorian painters included J. M. W. Turner, whose famous painting *Rain, Steam and Speed* (1844), is said to be of Brunel's masterpiece, Maidenhead Bridge (see Bridges, page 19); and Alfred Sisley, the landscape artist, who painted *Molesey Weir* and *Hampton Court Bridge* in 1854.

One of England's most famous 20th-century painters, Sir Stanley Spencer, spent most of his life in Cookham, drawing constant inspiration from the Thames in and around his native village. He painted a series of pictures of Cookham Regatta, and other works included *Swan Upping at Cookham*, *A View from Cookham Bridge* and *Bellrope Meadow*, through which the Thames Path passes (see page 132).

Natural Thames

The Thames is a majestic but essentially lowland river which meanders through a gentle landscape with few gradients. The one exception is where the river has carved a route through the chalk of the Chiltern Hills at Goring Gap to create some magnificent beech-clad hillsides which can be truly breathtaking in their autumn colours.

On your Thames Path walk you will pass through areas of woodland, watermeadows and pastures which form the main habitats along the Thames Valley. Meadows cut for hay and pasture grazed by livestock have been the traditional form of farming here for centuries and they contain a huge assortment of native grasses and herbs.

The richness of habitat is illustrated by the fact that there are 146 Sites of Special Scientific Interest (SSSIs) within 3 miles (5 km) of the river, while two National Nature Reserves lie along the Thames, at North Meadow near Cricklade and Chimney Meadows deep in the lonely country upstream from Oxford.

The wide range of grassland provides a haven for a fantastic variety of wild flowers and, depending on the time of year, a wonderful array can be spotted from the Thames Path. The beautiful but increasingly rare snake's head fritillary flowers in great profusion each April at North Meadow near Cricklade and also at Iffley Meadows in Oxford. The rare summer snowflake, or Loddon lily, also makes an appearance on a few upper Thames flood meadows in spring. Other species to be found include bright yellow clusters of marsh marigold, subtle pink cuckooflower, yellow flag iris, purple loosestrife, common valerian, ox-eyed daisies, cowslips and meadow buttercups.

In the summer months many interesting insects are to be seen buzzing around the flowers and plants along the river banks, including hosts of dragonflies and dramatic

North Meadow, Cricklade, in May offers the rare sight of snake's-head fritillary.

Hares can sometimes be seen in the meadows along the Thames.

blue damselflies. Butterflies found along the Thames include gatekeepers, meadow browns, ringlets and common blues.

The most familiar and easy-to-spot birds to be seen along or on the Thames are swans, geese, mallard ducks, great crested grebes, coots and herons. If you happen to be walking the path in July, you may get chance to observe the brightly coloured boats that take part in the ancient ceremony of 'swan upping'. This curious tradition, more than 600 years old, is the annual census of swans on the river, establishing the number belonging to the Crown and to two City Livery Companies, the Vintners and the Dyers.

A rare flash of bright blue streaking along the river bank close to the water could be to a kingfisher, while overhead you may spot buzzards, kestrels and red kites patrolling the skies. Closer to London you may even hear the exotic squawk of a ring-necked parakeet, as large numbers of these tropical birds are now thriving in our less than tropical climate.

Summer brings swallows, swifts, house and sand martins swooping and diving low over the water. The wetland meadows near to the river are home to ground-nesting birds like curlew, snipe and reed bunting.

Otters have been successfully introduced to the upper reaches of the Thames, but it is very difficult to spot these elusive creatures. Water voles are equally difficult to see, but although numbers are very low, they are recovering along some tributaries.

The aggressive American mink has been spotted along the river in increasing numbers. Where they can be trapped, the native species have a better chance of surviving. Away from the river, hares can be seen on the grass meadowlands.

Thames swans and cygnets are counted each July in the ancient ceremony of swan upping.

Thames locks and weirs

One very welcome sight that you'll regularly come across as you walk along the banks of the Thames is the humble lock. You will soon notice that most of them have a bench or two and several offer refreshments. All are manned, either full or part time, and the lock-keeper's cottage garden is usually very well kept, displaying a riot of colour in summer.

The locks and weirs have been built over the years to control the flow of water between the highest navigable point of the river at Lechlade (240 feet/73.1 metres above sea level) and the start of the tidal Thames at Teddington (13½ feet/4 metres above sea level). Their establishment has played a crucial part in the development of the Thames as a major transport route. Early travelling in and around the Thames Valley was hazardous on land, so people looked to the river as a means of transport. Generally speaking, water levels would have been too low in summer and too high in winter, so some sort of control was needed. Millers started to build rudimentary weirs to control the flow of water, but the problem was how to get a boat past these dams. In Elizabethan times water levels along the Thames were controlled by a series of flash-locks, or navigation weirs. The water was allowed to build up behind the weir until a boat could pass through, hauled by men on the way upstream, or, heading downstream, carried with the torrent of water as the gate was opened. These flash-locks, however, created dangerous currents and were a real hazard to the boats as they passed through. The last flash-lock on the Thames was finally removed at Eaton Hastings as recently as 1937.

In the early 17th century a new design called a 'pound lock' was introduced, based on a man-made chamber with heavy gates at each end. Early examples were located at Sandford, Iffley and Abingdon. The remainder of the 45 locks and associated weirs were then installed between 1772 and 1928, and to this day the pound lock system is the type of lock used on the Thames.

The early weirs were based on a 'paddle-and-rymer' system. Rymers are wooden posts and the paddles are slotted in between them to control the water flow. Five weirs today – at Northmoor, Rushey, Iffley, Goring and Streatley – still operate this system, although the Environment Agency is carrying out a modernisation and replacement programme.

Locks and weirs today

The Environment Agency manages the flow of water along the River Thames and is responsible for the upkeep of the locks and weirs between Cricklade and Teddington, where the river becomes tidal. The river is extremely popular with boat users, and all the locks below Godstow are hydraulically operated and all are manned at least part time. Weirs, too, have become popular with canoeists and kayakers, and a series of salmon ladders has been installed to help the fish travel upstream. Despite improved water-level management, regular winter flooding can occur anywhere along the Thames, but especially above Oxford. The Environment Agency Floodline has up-to-date information (see Useful Information, page 162).

Heading downstream from Lechlade, you will encounter 43 locks and associated weirs on your journey to Hampton Court. There are two further locks at Teddington and Richmond. Passing any lock adds interest and excitement to a riverside walk, but the following are particularly worth looking out for:

St John's Lock, near Lechlade The first lock you encounter on your Thames Path walk, just a short distance downstream from Lechlade. Here you will find the statue of Old Father Thames as he reclines and keeps an eye on passers-by at the highest navigable point on the river. He was originally installed at the very start of the Thames Path but relocated here due to problems of vandalism.

Buscot Lock, near Lechlade The smallest lock on the river and located in a wonderful rural setting. It is positioned conveniently close to the National Trust village of Buscot with its quaint shop and tea room and is a haven for wildlife.

Rushey Lock, near Tadpole Bridge Built in 1896 and a very good example of a manually operated pound lock. It is said that the lock-keeper's cottage used to be a guest house for Errol Flynn and Douglas Fairbanks. It has wonderfully well-kept gardens, complete with a topiary frog.

The associated Rushey Weir is an increasingly rare example of an old Thames paddle-and-rymer weir, which is now a listed structure. There are paddles stacked by the path, and you can see how they are dropped into place between the heavier posts with handles, the rymers, to hold the water back. Rushey Weir is due to be automated in 2013.

Godstow Lock, near Oxford A pound lock which, to protect the interests of the Trout Inn nearby, had a ruling that no refreshments could be provided. It was near here that Charles Dodgson, better known as Lewis Carroll, used to picnic with his friend Henry Liddell, whose daughter Alice Carroll immortalised in *Alice's Adventures in Wonderland* and *Through the Looking-Glass* (see Literary Thames, page 13).

Sandford Lock, near Oxford This lock and weir form a massive construction nicknamed the 'Sandford Lasher'. The lock has the highest fall of any on the river and the dangerous undercurrents of the weir pool have claimed many lives. Several Oxford college students have drowned here, as did the foster son of J. M. Barrie, author of *Peter Pan*.

Day's Lock, near Little Wittenham A pound lock built in 1789 by the Thames Navigation Commissioner, this is the main gauging station for measuring water flow down the river. It is also the place where the World Pooh Sticks Championships have taken place every year since 1983.

Mapledurham Lock and Mill, near Reading This lock dates from 1777 and was improved in 1908. It has been associated for centuries with a corn mill, which is still working to this day. Thus Mapledurham is the only Thames lock and weir combination with two functions.

Hambleden Lock and Weir, near Henley This was the location of an early mill and site of a flash-lock which was replaced with a pound lock in 1773. One of the first lock-keepers here, Caleb Gould, was a real

Looking back on the white waters after crossing the spectacular Benson Weir.

character. He served for 59 years and used to bake bread for the bargemen. His grave bears the famous epitaph: 'The world's a jest – and all things show it – I thought so once – and now I know it.'

Hambleden Lock was the start of the first Oxford and Cambridge Boat Race in 1829 and has also featured in a *Midsomer Murder* mystery. The rushing waters over the long weir make a very impressive sight.

Boulters Lock, near Maidenhead On the outskirts of the town, this is probably the best-known lock on the river. Built as a pound lock in 1772, it was made famous by Victorian boat parties due to its proximity to Cliveden, especially on the Sunday of the Royal Ascot race meeting. The weir makes a very popular kayaking venue and the last salmon ladder installed on the Thames was located here in 2000.

Thames bridges

Another regular feature of the path is the endless variety of bridges that you pass over or under on your Thames journey. In fact, there are about 90 bridges crossing the River Thames between its source and Hampton Court, ranging from ancient stone structures to sleek suspension and modern footbridges.

The oldest bridge?

Despite early Saxon foundations at Folly Bridge in Oxford (see page 68), Radcot Bridge claims to be the oldest on the Thames. This three-arched bridge was built of Taynton stone in the early 1200s and is a remarkable survivor: it was nearly destroyed in the Battle of Radcot Bridge in 1387 and again during the War of the Roses between 1455 and 1487. However, it has been argued that Radcot Bridge doesn't count as a proper Thames crossing, as it spans a side-channel and not the main river.

Newbridge, to the west of Oxford, despite its name, also claims the title of oldest bridge over the main Thames. It was built in 1250 by monks using the same Taynton stone as at Radcot and originally had 51 arches! (St Paul's Cathedral is also built of Taynton stone, quarried in the Cotswolds and carried to London by barges.) Incredibly, despite its age, Newbridge is still in use today, carrying the traffic on the A415 trunk road between Witney and Abingdon.

Famous bridge designers

Isambard Kingdom Brunel, the remarkable engineer of the Great Western Railway, designed three brick railway bridges over the Thames at Moulsford, Gatehampton and Maidenhead, and a further iron bridge at Windsor. His greatest challenge was the Maidenhead Bridge, which needed to span both the towpath and the navigation channel. Critics did not believe it was possible, but he came up with the longest, flattest brick arch in the world, measuring 128 feet (39 metres) across with a rise of just 24 feet (7.3 metres). His doubters were proved wrong, as the expresses still thunder across this magnificent bridge as they did in Brunel's day. It was probably this bridge that featured in J. M. W. Turner's painting *Rain, Steam and Speed* (see Artistic Thames, page 14).

Isambard Kingdom Brunel

Sir George Gilbert Scott, the famous Victorian architect of the Albert Memorial and the recently renovated Midland Hotel, St Pancras in London, came up with the stunning design for the Thames bridge at Clifton Hampden. The location of the bridge and its juxtaposition with Clifton Hampden church make for one of the most photographed views along the whole river.

Sir George Gilbert Scott

William Tierney Clark, a civil engineer, was the architect behind the graceful suspension bridge at Marlow, which was built in 1829–32. He had already achieved fame as a pioneering suspension bridge designer and his work included the original Hammersmith Bridge in 1824 (since replaced). His most renowned suspension bridge, however, is probably the elegant structure over the River Danube in Budapest.

Sir Edwin Lutyens, the great architect of country houses and war memorials, designed the Hampton Court Bridge. This is the fourth bridge to cross the Thames here and replaced an earlier iron span construction. The bridge was opened on 3 July 1933 by the Prince of Wales, for whom it was a remarkably busy day: he also opened new bridges over the Thames at Chiswick and Twickenham on the same day.

Sir Edwin Lutyens

Other interesting bridges

Toll bridges There were once many toll bridges over the Thames, but only two remain: at Swinford and Whitchurch. Luckily for walkers, the pedestrian tax at Swinford was abolished in 1835 and Whitchurch, which is on the Trail itself, is also free for those crossing on foot.

Pedestrians used to pay half a penny to cross the Thames by bridge at Lechlade. The charge was abolished in 1839 but the bridge, built in 1792, has retained the wonderful name of Ha'penny Bridge.

Canaletto's painting of 1754 shows the construction of Old Walton Bridge.

Abingdon Bridge This can be considered one of the wider bridges, but strictly speaking it is two bridges, which were required to cross the floodplain at this point. The original, built by the Fraternity of the Holy Cross in 1416, had 14 arches and its opening damaged trade to nearby Wallingford. Many improvements were made when Abingdon Lock opened in 1790 and, although largely rebuilt last century, the bridge has retained its medieval feel.

Sonning Bridge An attractive brick arch construction dating back to 1775. It is unfortunately too narrow for the demands of modern traffic, but it is strategically important as the only road crossing of the River Thames between Reading and Henley. It has been a favourite subject for artists. Dick Turpin, the highwayman, was reputedly a regular user of Sonning Bridge, over which he used to make his rapid escapes from the authorities. His aunt lived in Sonning village nearby.

Henley Bridge An elegant five-arched stone bridge built in 1786 which has created another pleasing river composition. Its location is an ancient crossing point, possibly dating back to Roman times. Look out for the keystones on either side of the bridge's central arch. On the upstream side is the figure of Isis and on the downstream side is Thamesis, by the sculptor Anne Seymour Damer.

Walton Bridge Although ordinary-looking today and in the process of being replaced, this crossing has a fascinating history. One of the most famous wooden bridges across the Thames outside London was constructed here in 1750. It was designed by William Etheridge in a similar way to the 'Mathematical Bridge' over the River Cam in Cambridge, which still stands today. The wooden bridge boasted the widest unsupported span in England, but survived only until 1783; however, it can be seen in all its glory in Canaletto's painting *Old Walton Bridge* (see Artistic Thames, page 14).

Thames islands

People walking along the Thames Path may not really notice the islands – sometimes called 'aits' or 'eyots' – in the river as they pass by. Because of the way the river flows and the system of locks and weirs, it is difficult to calculate their precise number. However, it is generally agreed that there are over 70 between Oxford and Hampton Court, so there are plenty of islands of all shapes and sizes to try to identify, some of which have been created artificially to aid navigation.

When walking downstream on the Thames Path from Oxford to Hampton Court the following – listed in the order in which you will pass them – are some of the more interesting:

Lock Wood Island, at Nuneham A regular haunt of Charles Dodgson, better known as Lewis Carroll, who came here with friends, including the young Alice Liddell. This location may have inspired him to write his *Alice's Adventures in Wonderland* and *Through the Looking-Glass* (see Literary Thames, page 13).

Fry's Island, or De Montfort Island, near Caversham This was the site of a famous duel that took place in 1163 between Robert de Montfort, a nobleman, and Henry of Essex, standard-bearer to Henry II. The duel was called by the king, as Robert had accused Henry of cowardice for dropping the Royal Standard during a battle with the Welsh. Watched by thousands of people, the contest took place while the royal court was in temporary residence in nearby Reading. Henry of Essex was the loser, but survived and later became a monk at Reading Abbey.

Temple Island, near Henley On a beautiful reach of the river, this island is famous for its role as the starting point for the races which make up in the Henley Regattas (see page 120). It is named after the temple or folly built on the island by James Wyatt in 1771 as a fishing lodge. It is the earliest example of ornamentation known as the Etruscan style.

Monkey Island, near Bray Named after the monks of a nearby monastery rather than the animal, the island has a famous hotel which was built for the 3rd Duke of Marlborough in 1745. It became very popular with royalty during the early 1900s, with Edward VII amongst its regular visitors. The writer H. G. Wells was also a frequent client.

Friday's Island, near Windsor A simple two-bedroomed cottage on this island was for 30 years the home of Julius Grant, a famous forensic scientist and forgery exposer, who proved in 1984 that the Hitler diaries were a fake.

Magna Carta Island, near Runnymede A possible location for the actual signing of the Magna Carta in 1215. It is known that the island was also the meeting place of Henry III and Louis, soon to be Louis VIII of France, in 1217.

Pharaoh's Island, near Shepperton This island was presented to Lord Nelson as a thank-you gift after the Battle of the Nile in 1798. He used it as a fishing retreat. There are a large number of residences on the island, but it is accessible only by boat. Sadly, two people drowned near here in 2011 when a dinghy capsized.

D'Oyly Carte Island, near Weybridge Richard D'Oyly Carte, the famous Victorian impresario and hotelier, lived on the island in a large mansion called Eyot House. He had hoped to run the house as a hotel along the lines of the Savoy in London, but was refused a licence. It is rumoured that Gilbert and Sullivan were regular visitors.

Platts Eyot, near Hampton Famous for boat building, with Tom Tagg (see Tagg's Island) opening a boatyard at the east end of the island in 1868. Coastal motor boats were built here in the First World War and motor torpedo boats and landing craft in the Second. Vosper Thornycroft subsequently took over the works, which closed in the 1960s.

Tagg's Island, near Hampton This island, with its houseboat community, is named after Tom Tagg, a 19th-century entrepreneur who hired out boats and built the Thames Hotel here in 1872. The hotel became a favourite with London Society, and the actress Sarah Bernhardt, amongst others, was a regular visitor. The island was subsequently bought by the famous theatre impresario Fred Karno in 1912; he rebuilt the hotel, naming it The Karsino. This 'island resort' was extremely popular with returning troops during and after the First World War, but after some financial problems Karno sold the hotel in 1926. It never regained its early success and was eventually demolished in the 1970s. However, one legacy of Fred Karno remains to this day. In 1911 he had a houseboat built which he was determined to make the best houseboat on the river. Named the *Astoria*, it could easily hold a full 90-piece orchestra. You can still see the *Astoria* in all her glory, moored on the north bank of the Thames near Hampton Court. It is now owned by Pink Floyd guitarist Dave Gilmour, who uses it as a floating recording studio.

...vans rest opposite the magnificent Astoria ...useboat moored on the Thames near Hampton.

Thames Path signs have the familiar acorn symbol to reassure walkers.

Introduction

Practical advice

Terrain

Your walk may be by a modest field path, just visible in the grass of the river bank, or along a broad and popular promenade. But at almost every point the Thames Path provides easy-going travel, with no call for specialist gear, except perhaps after prolonged rain in the upper reaches, when wellies are advisable on a short walk along a soggy towpath. However, you should be aware that in most winters there is regular flooding of the upper reaches and the Path shouldn't be attempted in these circumstances. For further information on flooding, please contact the Environment Agency Floodline (see Useful Information, page 162). Generally the clay and gravel of the Thames Valley will compact underfoot when dry, making a pleasant walking surface through most seasons, and the work of volunteer teams keeps the riverside path clear of summer foliage.

Downstream or upstream?

Of course, the Thames Path can be walked in either direction. In this book we have chosen to describe it in the downstream direction, in part because many people find it easier to read maps from left to right and most of the time your back will be to the prevailing wind, but also because of the gradually growing sense of climax as you follow the river down towards London.

Signposting

As on the other National Trails, you can expect to find that the route is well signed with 'Thames Path' and the familiar National Trail acorns. Many fingerposts also indicate the distance to the next main access point along the walk, and there are Thames Path information points at 19 locks, not only reminding you of the route but also giving extra information about nearby features and places of interest. Along the rural Thames many new riverside paths have been created, but this work is ongoing and there are still a couple of points where you have to follow a temporary route away from the river. The maps identify these temporary stretches, and when you come to the start of one it is advisable to look around for new 'Thames Path' signs that will guide you to a recently created section. The signing will always guide you along the best route currently available, so keep alert for possible changes. The Thames Path website www.nationaltrail.co.uk/thamespath has an up-to-date list of closures and diversions along the route.

Using the Thames Path

The old Thames towpath was used by men and horses to tow barges, but despite this tradition it should be noted that its legal status is only that of a public footpath. So it must be stressed that, although there are a few short bridleway sections (easily identifiable on the maps) and stretches with either formal or informal cycleway status, in general the Thames Path is a National Trail for walkers.

Remember, too, that throughout the rural Thames your walk is through farming land, so keep to the riverside path, resist the urge to take short-cuts across the meadows, and be sure to leave gates as you find them. You will often meet anglers, and at times their gear tends to spread across the towpath, so be tolerant and step quietly and carefully around them. Boating parties frequently stop and picnic, placing their mooring lines where they might trip you up – another case for cheerful tolerance.

In truth, Old Father Thames seems to pass on his genial good nature to all his followers. The boating family will give you a wave as they pass, the lock-keeper will usually have time for a chat as you pause to admire his flowerbeds. If there is one piece of essential advice for the Thames Path walker, it must surely be – don't hurry!

Responsibility for the Thames Path

As mentioned, the Thames Path was designated a National Trail by the Countryside Agency (now Natural England) and opened in 1996. A team of National Trail staff is mainly funded by Natural England, but some posts are part-funded by the highway authorities and all are employed by Oxfordshire County Council to manage theTrail.

Natural England also funds most of the maintenance work. Much of the important practical work, such as monitoring the route, litter-collecting, signposting and vegetation clearance, is carried out by enthusiastic members of the National Trails Volunteer Scheme, under the supervision of National Trail staff.

Other walks

The Thames Path crosses one National Trail, The Ridgeway (87 miles/139km from Overton Hill near Avebury to Ivinghoe Beacon near Tring) at Streatley, and there are two other National Trails nearby. Close to the source in the Cotswolds is the Cotswold Way National Trail (102 miles/164 km from Chipping Campden to Bath); and the Thamesdown Link connects the Thames Path at Kingston to the North Downs Way National Trail (153 miles/245 km from Farnham to Dover) at Westhumble near Dorking. Official National Trail Guides to all three are published by Aurum Press in the same series as this book.

There are many other excellent waymarked walks along the Thames Valley that link to the Thames Path. From the source you will encounter the following routes: the Wysis Way (Kemble to Monmouth); the d'Arcy Dalton Way (Wormleighton, Warwickshire, to Wayland's Smithy via Radcot Bridge); Shakespeare's Way (Stratford-upon-Avon to London via Oxford, Marlow and Cookham); the Oxford Canal Walk (Oxford to Coventry); the Kennet and Avon Towpath (Reading to Bath); the Oxfordshire Way (Bourton on the Water to Henley); the Chiltern Way (a circular walk through the Chilterns at Marlow); the Beeches Way (Cookham to West Drayton); and the Three Castles Path (Windsor to Winchester Castle Hall).

The section of Thames Path from Oxford to Weybridge is also designated as part of the E2 European walking route, which runs from Galway to Nice.

A narrowboat makes its way through the picturesque lock at Goring.

Thames Path
in the Country

Source to Cricklade

via Neigh Bridge Country Park and Ashton Keynes
12¼ miles (19.7 km)

This first section provides a gentle introduction to the Thames Path National Trail. Users generally start from Kemble station, which is near the trail but a mile or so from the source; as a result they end up walking this first part twice. These early stages are invariably along a dry river bed, but the waters of the infant river are soon encountered. After passing through the hamlet of Ewen and the larger village of Ashton Keynes, surrounded by the endless lakes of the Cotswold Water Park, the walk finishes by crossing the vast openness of North Meadow to arrive at the attractive little town of Cricklade. This section is especially rewarding in spring when the wild flowers of North Meadow will be at their finest.

Transport options

After the ease of reaching Kemble by train, you are then dependent on infrequent buses. A 7-mile (11.3-km) walk from the source brings you to Ashton Keynes, where there is an occasional bus service to Swindon on weekdays, while Cricklade has a more regular service, including Saturdays.

Things to look out for

1 Source of the Thames The river's birthplace is open to dispute, but is generally accepted as being a spring that rises in a field called Trewsbury Mead a few miles from Cirencester (see box). It is located under an ancient ash tree and marked with a simple stone carved by the Thames Conservators. For 16 years up to 1974, Old Father Thames himself resided here to greet you, but today he reclines in greater security at St John's Lock near Lechlade; you will pass him later.

2 Lyd Well This ancient spring is marked by a grove of trees and the retaining wall of a pond, but after a period of rain this is where the very first Thames water will gush up from a little grassy dell.

3 Kemble The nearest settlement to the source of the River Thames, Kemble was once an important railway junction. The Golden Valley Line from Swindon to Cheltenham passes through the village, and branch lines from Cirencester and Tetbury met here. Although the branch lines were dismantled in the 1960s, Kemble railway station is still important for passengers travelling from Cirencester to Swindon and London.

Cotswold Airport (previously known as Kemble Airport) on the edge of the village was once home to the Red Arrows aerobatic display team. The airfield is now used by light industry and flying clubs, and has two annual air displays.

4 **Somerford Keynes** Since AD 685 there has been a Christian settlement on this site, just a short walk from the Thames Path. For centuries Somerford Keynes was a Wiltshire village but in 1897 it voted to be in Gloucestershire. It has many fine listed buildings, including the Manor House near All Saints Church, and walkers may like to detour to the Bakers Arms.

5 **Cotswold Water Park** This huge area of land has, over the last 50 years, been transformed from gravel-pit workings into a series of about 150 lakes to form the Cotswold Water Park. It is managed by a trust to ensure that the wildlife and biodiversity of the lakes are protected whilst offering a range of water-based recreational activities. Many walking trails are being developed to allow further exploration of this transformed area.

6 **Ashton Keynes** This attractive village was described by William Cobbett in 1826 as 'a very curious place', as the Thames passes through it in a series of channels. Curious maybe, but there are many beautiful old buildings of Cotswold stone to enjoy, as well as the four inexplicable headless preaching crosses dotted around. Why the village had so many is a mystery, but the church is appropriately called Holy Cross. In addition to the White Hart and the Horse and Jockey pubs, there is also a village shop where walkers can stock up on provisions.

7 **North Meadow Nature Reserve** Established here in 1973, North Meadow protects one of the finest remaining examples of ancient lowland hay meadow in Europe. It is a National Nature Reserve and a Special Area of Conservation, yet is still open to common grazing on the old Lammas Land principle. Among the many wild flower rarities to be seen here, towards the end of April each year is the best display anywhere of the beautiful snake's-head fritillary.

Cirencester

This attractive town, known as 'the Capital of the Cotswolds', is served by train from Kemble station and is only a few miles from the start of the walk. It is well worth a visit. It was once the most important Roman town outside London and artefacts from this period can be viewed in the Corinium Museum. It also boasted the second largest Augustinian foundation in the country and grew rich on the Cotswold wool trade, which is most famously celebrated in the magnificence of the huge parish church of St John the Baptist.

Cirencester is famous for its agricultural college, the oldest established college of this type in the English-speaking world.

The distinctive roofline of Blackjack Street in old Cirencester

Route description

Although the source of the Thames lies, seemingly, in a remote Gloucestershire meadow, it is in truth only a short walk from Kemble station **A**. So your walk of discovery will very likely begin at the station forecourt on the London-bound side, taking the approach road to join another road. Turn left here, and, in just 75 yards (70 metres), a path signed the Wysis Way (a 55-mile/88-km link route between the Offa's Dyke and Thames Path National Trails) on the right crosses a stile to follow a stream that sometimes flows into the infant Thames but which can, like the Thames itself, be just a dry dip in the meadow in summer. Just to assert that it is sometimes a vigorous little tributary, a footbridge crosses just before it enters the main stream. Turn left over this bridge **B** to join the Thames Path and follow the left bank of the Thames for a while up a broad valley, the course of the river quite apparent even when dry. Soon the right of way climbs to the left-hand side of the field through two gates.

When you see, opposite, a big house of Cotswold stone, take the path bearing right across the meadow. In the dip, you can easily trace the line where an infant Thames occasionally flows, and even the tumble of stones that was once a footbridge. Ahead, you can see the traffic on the Roman Fosse Way; from here aim for a flight of stone steps leading up to a gate. Cross the road cautiously – the traffic is fast here – then continue down a farm approach opposite, through a gate on the right, and carry on along a track with a fence to your left. The track goes through a gate in the long stone wall ahead and you keep on by a faint track marked by

Autumn colours reflect in the still waters of an infant Thames on the approach to Ashton Keynes.

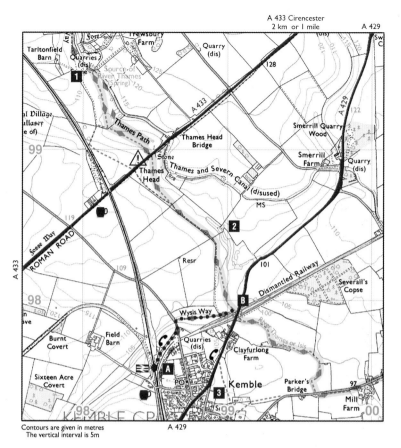

A 429

A 433 Cirencester
2 km or 1 mile

31

Source to Cricklade

a straggly line of trees; ahead, the tower of Coates Church acts as a useful guide. One more gate and you are there – the pebbles of the head spring beneath an elderly ash tree, the simple stone placed by the Thames Conservators, and a signpost to confirm that this is the **source of the Thames** ❶, and your walk truly starts here.

So, suitably inspired, and in the certain knowledge that it must all be downhill from here on, you set out back along the track towards Kemble, along the line of trees, via the gate and the clear path back across the Fosse Way. After a wet season, the bowl of grass to your left can be a lake of Thames water, fed by the

first spring known as the **Lyd Well** ❷. The right of way climbs to the right-hand field boundary for a while, but, towards the end of the field, you should branch left again to find the Thames channel. Again cross the small footbridge, but turn left through the gate beside the two-arch bridge that takes it under the road into **Kemble** village ❸. Just to the right, across the road, go through a gate and carry on along a rough path by the river bank, the Thames now to your right, with the spire of Kemble Church visible over the fields beyond. Coming up to Parker's Bridge, bear left and cross the road to take the little path that wends its way along the green strip between river and road. When it gives up, keep on along the road into the farms and cottages of Ewen. Ahead, through the village, is the picturesque Wild Duck Inn.

📖 *To visit the Wild Duck Inn, keep ahead through the village for 440 yards (400 metres), forking left at the second junction. The pub will be found on the right.*

But your route turns right at the first road junction in Ewen. On the outskirts of the village and immediately after crossing the Thames, turn left through a gate **C**. Now the path keeps along the river bank, leading through a kissing-gate into open meadows and on under the crackling power lines to Upper Mill Farm. So modest is the flow of water here, it is difficult to believe that it worked watermills, yet your path passes by the one-time mill race, turning left in another 25 yards (20 metres) through a kissing-gate to take a footbridge over the mill stream **D**. Once over, go through another kissing-gate and turn right to follow the field boundary, now with the Thames to your right. Cross a plank footbridge, with Somerford Keynes in view over the fields, turn right again and continue by the river past Old Mill Farm. In the next big field, the serene grouping of church and Manor House of **Somerford Keynes 4** is visible just a field or two to your left.

Somerford Lakes are most likely to be the first water you will encounter on your walk.

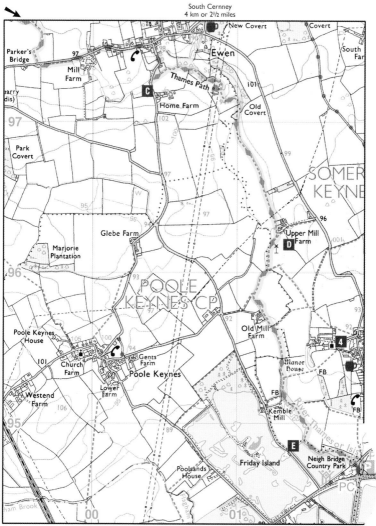

South Cernney
4 km or 2½ miles

Contours are given in metres
The vertical interval is 5m

3 km or 2 miles
Oaksey

▶ *To visit Somerford Keynes and the Bakers Arms, take the footpath to the left across the fields to the village.*

The Thames Path keeps by the field edge through several kissing-gates until a long, wooden footbridge **E** takes it into Neigh Bridge Country Park.

Here, even if your walk so far has been by a stubbornly dry Thames, you will find a lake full of water, an inviting spot to take a lakeside stroll or stop for a picnic. Turn left after crossing the bridge and continue on the path by the riverside until you finally come up to the lane by Neigh Bridge itself.

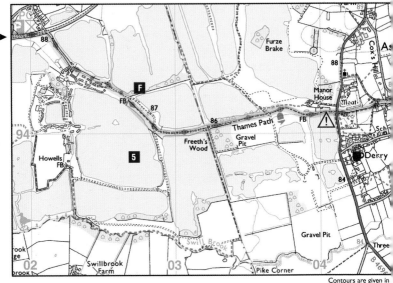

B 4696

Contours are given in
The vertical interval

Cross the lane and turn right to walk on the grass verge, then left along the broad Spine Road of the **Cotswold Water Park** 5. You will go over the Thames again in another 150 yards (135 metres), then cross the road to take the gravel path beside the lane opposite. Very soon you are looking over Mill Lake to your left, as the Thames appears beside you again to your right. Beyond the Lower Mill Estate housing, keep on by the broad track where you will now see even more water to the right – Lower Mill Nature Reserve.

Just before the track comes to the gate into Farmhouse Lake, take the footbridge over the Thames F, turn left and continue, with the river now on your left, towards Ashton Keynes. After the vast, watery expanses, the sylvan path through Flood Hatches Copse comes as a complete contrast. Passing a quarry on the right, keep ahead

through two kissing-gates with the river still on your left. The Thames follows several courses through and around **Ashton Keynes** 6, and you will cross one channel via a wooden footbridge flowing away to the right before the path crosses a road. Take care crossing the road and keep ahead to the village centre.

▶ *To visit the Horse and Jockey pub, take the footpath on the right soon after crossing the road.*

The path squeezes ahead between cottages into a charming village scene. A mini-Thames flows in its stone-edged channel across the grass and under an equally diminutive bridge – the glow of Cotswold stone all around. Walking ahead to the road you will pass one of the four preaching crosses in Ashton Keynes – headless but ancient. Holy Cross Church is reached by a path leading away behind you.

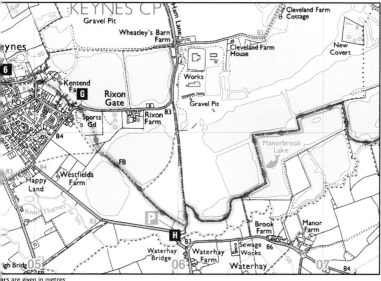

*rs are given in metres
*ertical interval is 5m

To visit the other village pub, the White Hart, turn right in the road, past the cross.

The Thames Path itself turns left in the road, then right down Back Street. This quiet lane leads to the right into Kent End to cross a little watercourse, and you go immediately left into the Kentend Farm drive. At the farm gates, go right through a kissing-gate and along the field edge with the water channel to the right. Through another kissing-gate, bear left with the path until you come to a drive that passes several houses and leads up to a road.

For the next half-mile (800 metres) to Waterhay, the Thames Path crosses an area transformed by recent gravel workings. Across the road to your left, go through a gate **G** into a sports field, cross their drive to a kissing-gate, then continue straight ahead with the pavilion to your right. A further gate

leads out of the sports field and across Ashton Keynes Millennium Green to take a causeway between two lakes. Once, this path followed a minor channel of the Thames, but you would not realize this today – the quarrying has ruthlessly swallowed it up. At Waterhay you join a more firmly established crossing way **H**, where you turn first left, then right. Take heed of the 'Danger Quicksand' signs as this bridleway winds its way through the Cleveland Lakes, more of the Cotswold Water Park. The first great water expanse on the right is Manorbrook Lake, part of which is devoted to fishing. Your way turns left to follow its bank, the waterscape around you becoming quite attractive as nature softens the rawness of former gravel workings. Several turns later, you finally leave Manorbrook through a gate. Carry on for a few yards, then turn right to skirt one more lake, Cleveland Lake.

Away to the left is Hailstone Hill, a point to aim for. Turning towards the hill, you will be pleasantly surprised to discover that you have joined the Thames again, flowing now just to your right under old Bournelake Farm bridge. But this is only a brief encounter before the bridleway swings away to the left, eventually coming to a gate and interpretation panel for Cleveland Lakes. Your journey continues to the right  over a bridge leading down to a broader crossing track, where you turn left.

At the next junction, turn right by an interpretation panel for Elmlea Meadow on a track that turns up on to the converted bed of the railway that once served Cricklade. Turn right and after 120 yards (100 metres), with a bridge clearly visible ahead, turn left through a gate to follow a track down to the riverside. Follow the river, first on the track, then on a meadow path until you reach another bridge on the line of the North Wiltshire Canal, which crossed the Thames here by a low aqueduct. By the bridge, a gate and steps lead left down into the vast, open vista of **North Meadow Nature Reserve** **7** with the river on your right.

Follow the river bank now past several gates, with the magnificent tower of St

Contours are given in
The vertical interval

Sampson's Church ahead, the focal point of several river compositions. After you have passed a gauging station, go through a gate and cross the river over a farm bridge **J**. Walk up the track and around a bend, keeping to the left-hand gated path, then left over a plank footbridge and on by a fenced path. Keep ahead through a gate and over an open field to an old metal kissing-gate and the first houses of Cricklade, where immediately you turn left along an estate path. Where the path, Bailiff's Piece, turns right, keep on through a gate in the hedge and head straight across an open and obviously popular meadow. Several paths aim for the far end, where a gate leads into a road, North Wall, and thus to the foot of Cricklade High Street. Turn right here to continue on the Thames Path and also to explore ☐☞🚌 Cricklade town centre.

An infant Thames runs shyly through its meadows, near Waterhay Bridge.

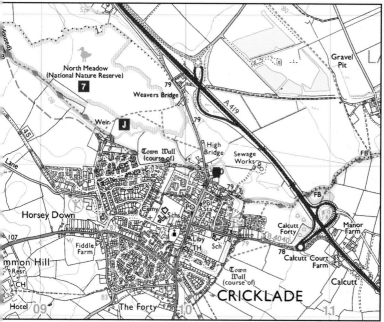

urs are given in metres
ertical interval is 5m

Public transport

Kemble (0.2 mile / 0.3 km) ⇌
Ashton Keynes (on route) 🚌 (weekdays only)
Cricklade (on route) 🚌 (not Sundays)
Taxis/minicabs: Cirencester, Siddington, Swindon

Refreshments and toilets

Thames Head (0.2 mile / 0.3 km) 🍺 Thames Head Inn
Kemble (0.5 mile /0.8 km) 🍺 Tavern Inn
Ewen (on route) 🍺 Wild Duck
Somerford Keynes (0.3 mile /0.5 km) 🍺 Bakers Arms
Ashton Keynes (on route) 🍺 White Hart, Horse and Jockey
Cricklade (on route) 🍺 wide selection; ☕ Cricklade Café
Food shops: Ashton Keynes, Cricklade
Public toilets: Cricklade

Accommodation

Cirencester (3 miles / 5 km) wide selection – contact Visitor Information Centre
Coates (1.3 miles / 2.1 km) Tunnel House Inn
Thames Head (0.2 mile / 0.3 km) Thames Head Inn
Kemble (0.5 mile / 0.8 km) Forge House, The Willows
Ewen (on route) Well Cottage, Wild Duck, Brooklands Farm
South Cerney (2 miles / 3.2 km) Eliot Arms, Meadow Cottage, Tanners
Ashton Keynes (on route) Wheatley's Farm, Cove House, The Longhouse
Latton (1.6 miles / 2.6 km) The Dolls House
Cricklade (on route) Cricklade House, Red Lion, Vale Hotel, White Hart Hotel, Upper Chelworth Farm

Walking this section you will see the reed-filled river slowly growing in size, but it is only as you approach Lechlade that the first boats can be spotted. After leaving Cricklade you will pass through empty countryside and occasional remote villages, such as Castle Eaton. Beyond Castle Eaton the route is generally away from the river and includes a temporary section of over 1 mile (1.6 km) along the side of the busy A361 trunk road. Please note that this section is best negotiated by taxi or bus (for information, see box page 43). The final stretch into Lechlade along the banks of the river provides much welcome relief.

Transport options

Castle Eaton after 4½ miles (7.2 km) and Upper Inglesham on the A361 are the only staging points on this walk. There is one bus each way between Castle Eaton and Swindon on Saturdays only. A bus service operates between Swindon and Lechlade daily (except Sundays) from Upper Inglesham.

Things to look out for

1 Cricklade and its churches The first township on the Thames, Cricklade, like many on the route, seems to have begun as a favoured crossing point. The Roman Ermine Street crosses nearby and, ironically, Cricklade's much-needed bypass has restored the Roman line. From the town bridge over the Thames, the High Street climbs steadily, with that marvellous English country-town mix of styles and periods, all living harmoniously together. St Sampson's Church stands back behind the houses and, while its massive Tudor tower with four great corner pinnacles dominates the meadows for miles around, it can hardly be seen from the High Street. Very visible, however, is the smaller, much-restored Norman church of St Mary, which has, most unusually, been rededicated as Cricklade's Catholic church. In its churchyard is a fine 14th-century preaching cross with figures in a four-sided lantern head.

2 Castle Eaton village and church As you pass through the small village of Castle Eaton, look out on the left-hand side for a stone-roofed lych-gate which leads to the church poised on the bank of the Thames. An 1860s restoration added a little bell turret with spire on the nave roof, a distinctive feature presumably intended to hold a Sanctus bell. The Red Lion Inn in the village is the first of many pubs to be found on the banks of the River Thames.

3 Kempsford Church The tall tower of St Mary's, Kempsford, is clearly visible across the river from the Thames Path. This ancient village was the birthplace of John Arkell, who founded Arkell's Brewery, and is well worth a visit.

4 Inglesham Church St John the Baptist Church at Inglesham is a marvellous little building that served a now almost vanished village. In Victorian times, thanks to William Morris, it was restored to its earlier character rather than suffering the Victorian Gothic treatment of other churches. So here you have a kind of time capsule, a parish church of a bygone era, with venerable 13th-century stonework, wall paintings and texts, a Jacobean pulpit and box pews. It is tended by the Churches Conservation Trust and, except at certain times of year when altar furnishings are in place, you should find it open.

5 Thames–Severn Canal At Roundhouse Farm near Lechlade the Thames–Severn Canal left the river to carry its trade, via the Sapperton Tunnel and Golden Valley, down to Stroud. One of the most ambitious of canal concepts, the waterway was completed in 1789 and at the time Sapperton Tunnel, at 2.17 miles (3.49 km), was the longest canal tunnel ever built. However, it was never really successful: water leaked constantly from its summit level and the last boat to travel between the Severn and the Thames did so in 1927. The roundhouses were the unusual quarters for lock-keepers and several survive to this day, although much of the canal is now dry.

The church of St Mary, Castle Eaton, stands by the bank of a reed-filled Thames, where even the smallest boats seldom try to navigate.

Route description

After visiting the town of **Cricklade 1**, you will find the Thames Path leaving the High Street eastwards, almost opposite St Mary's Church, via Abingdon Court Lane. Where the lane turns right, go sharp left into a drive. Arriving at a point where the ways divide into several directions, squeeze through a gap in the hedge on the right where there are steps going over a large stone slab. Turn left and follow the fence to a hedge gap leading into open meadows, once more by the Thames, now swollen by the waters of the Churn and soon by other tributaries, the Key and the Ray. Cross the first of these by means of a concrete farm bridge, then turn left and follow the Thames bank through a gate, under the bypass and on to Eysey footbridge **A**. At this pretty spot you cross the Thames itself and take to paths along its north bank. Walk on through the riverside meadows, now beneath the gentle slope of tree-clad Eysey Hill, through several gates and a length of path through dense foliage to reach the lonely Water Eaton Footbridge **B**.

Once over the footbridge, turn left to follow the river bank with the barns of Water Eaton Farm up on your right. The riverside path from here into Castle Eaton was created specially for Thames Path walkers. It crosses a succession of double-gated footbridges over water channels, one of them with a venerable willow of awe-inspiring size nearby, still displaying a defiant flourish of greenery. After running through open meadows the path goes through a plantation of young trees that comes down to the river. Then, after following the meanders of the Thames through several vast meadows, the path brings you to within sight of the cottages of **Castle Eaton 2** up ahead. As you

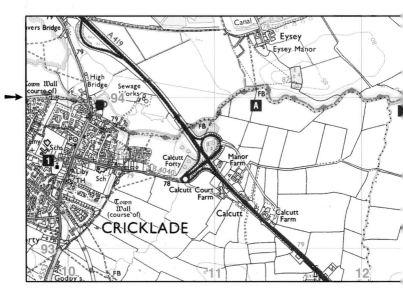

approach the village a faint track leads off to the right, away from the river, to a footbridge and kissing-gate leading to the foot of Mill Lane.

Walk on up the lane, with houses on either side, and keep ahead in The Street **C**. Follow it past mellow stone cottages to the large Georgian inn, 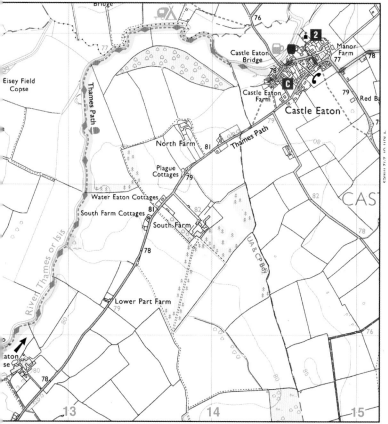 the Red Lion. *Just before the inn, a quick diversion left down the Kempsford road will give you a glimpse of the river.*

But the route from here is not by the river, so keep on, turning right by the big barns of Manor Farm. Continue

rs are given in metres
ertical interval is 5m

Bygone Canals

Just west of Cricklade, the quiet hamlet of Latton used to be a major canal junction. Here the North Wiltshire Canal, which opened in 1819, linked the Thames–Severn Canal with the Wilts–Berks Canal until its closure in 1927. Ambitious plans are being made to restore these defunct waterways.

ahead into Long Row, named after the terrace of cottages on your right. At the end of the road turn left into Church View and follow the road round a right-hand bend before turning left again into a farm lane leading to Blackford Farm. Follow this quiet lane round several bends, then, after passing some barns on your left, carry on until you pass the little farmhouse itself on the right. Walk on over the grass, then left **D** to follow the field boundary down to another brief meeting with the Thames. The river here is a reedy channel, with farms and the tall, graceful tower of **Kempsford Church** **3** just over the meadows beyond. Your path follows the Thames bank, then a side channel, through several gates and into a lane opposite cottages at Hannington Bridge.

Turn right and continue until, where the lane turns right at a junction of ways, you turn left on to a track that leads to a house. Just before reaching

this, fork right **E** on to the start of the fine bridlepath to Upper Inglesham. For 1½ miles (2.4 km) this rolls along with, for the most part, a ditch and hedge to the left and open fields to the right. The Thames is just a field or two away but out of sight. Eventually a bridlegate leads to a ford over a tributary stream, with a footbridge just to the right. Cross and walk forward 50 yards (45 metres) into the corner of a field **F**; here turn right and walk with the boundary hedge on your right up to the cottages of Upper Inglesham. On this field, you can easily see the lines of medieval ridge-and-furrow cultivation, first parallel to your route, then running across it. This was the result of using non-reversible ploughs on the same strip of land over time. Coming into the lane, turn left up to the A361 road, and then left again. Ahead lies over a mile of busy road: **please see the information box opposite about this part of the route.**

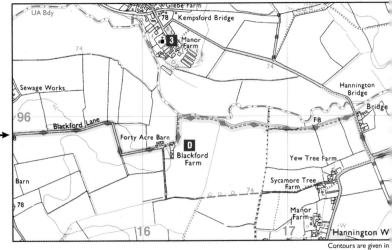

Contours are given in
The vertical interval

Important information about the A361 between Upper Inglesham and Inglesham

The section of Thames Path between Upper Inglesham and Inglesham is best negotiated by taxi (try taxis in Lechlade on 01367 252575 or 01367 253424). An alternative is to flag down bus services 64 or 74 heading north on the A361 at Upper Inglesham and take them to Lechlade. There are several bus services each day except Sunday, when there are none. Visit the South West pages of Traveline on www.traveline.info or call them on 0871 200 2233 for up-to-date information. Walkers can choose to walk along the 1 mile (1.6 km) of A361, but the speed limit is 60mph, there's a blind bend and the road has to be crossed at the start and finish. Part

of this stretch does have a pavement, but elsewhere there is a grass verge on the east side which is narrow in places. Managers of the Thames Path are actively working with landowners to finalise the path's route closer to the river, so make sure you follow the signs on the ground as the map here may be out of date.

The simple but magnificent church at Inglesham.

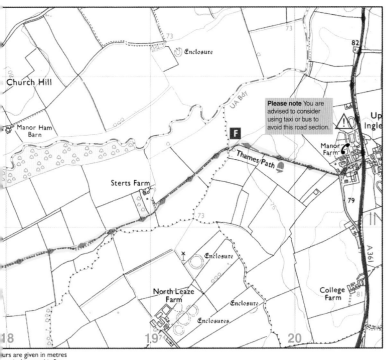

Please note You are advised to consider using taxi or bus to avoid this road section.

Contours are given in metres
vertical interval is 5m

At the end of this busy road section you can turn with relief down the lane signposted to **Inglesham Church 4**. To visit this very attractive little church, don't turn right following the Thames Path signs but continue ahead to the end of the lane. Afterwards retrace your steps up the lane a little until a kissing-gate **G** takes you into the meadows towards Lechlade. Walk diagonally left across the field until you reach a footbridge by the Thames. Don't cross it, but follow the bank around the first bend, where you will see a stone-built farmhouse and behind it an odd roundhouse – Roundhouse Farm, where you will find what remains today of the **Thames–Severn Canal 5**, which once branched off from the river.

You have reached an important landmark on your walk. On the bank opposite the farmhouse is a modest block of stone, the abutment of a bridge that brought the canal towpath over the Thames to your feet, from where it follows the river down to Putney. From here on, it will provide many days of easy walking by the Thames. So, set off with a new assurance through a gate and over a footbridge into Lechlade's riverside park and continue ahead to the 18th-century Town Bridge, usually called Ha'penny Bridge from the toll once charged. An archway with gate will take you ahead towards St John's Lock, but you may wish to cross the bridge and explore 🅿 🍴 🚆 Lechlade.

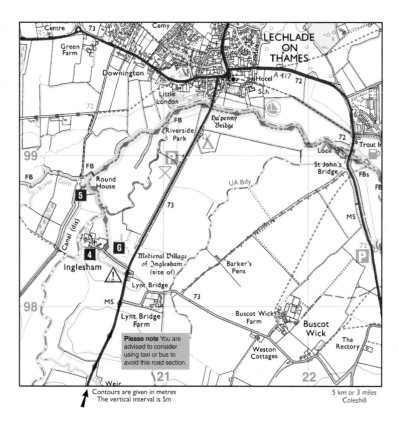

Contours are given in metres
The vertical interval is 5m

5 km or 3 miles
Coleshill

The river winds gracefully across the flood plain at St John's Lock, Lechlade.

Public transport

Castle Eaton (on route) 🚌 (Saturdays only)
Upper Inglesham (on route) 🚌 (not Sundays)
Lechlade (on route) 🚌
Taxis/minicabs: Lechlade

Refreshments and toilets

Castle Eaton (on route) 🍺 Red Lion
Lechlade (on route) 🍺 good range;
☕ Black Cat Tea Rooms
Food shops: Cricklade, Lechlade
Public toilets: Cricklade, Lechlade

Accommodation

Castle Eaton (on route) Red Lion, The Lodge
Marston Meysey (2.4 miles/3.9 km) Second Chance Touring Park campsite
Kempsford (1.1 miles/1.8 km) Kempsford Manor
Upper Inglesham (on route) Evergreen
Lechlade (on route) Cambrai Lodge, Park End Wharf, New Inn, The Crown, Bridge House Camp Site (closed November–March)

3 Lechlade to Newbridge

via Kelmscott and the remote Tadpole Bridge
16¾ miles (26.7 km)

This section truly is the River Thames at its remotest. Be prepared, because once you leave Lechlade you will not pass another village or shop on this section. There are, however, two pubs on the route and one nearby in Kelmscott village. The river meanders endlessly through open and empty countryside and the first locks appear – a welcome and colourful sight, especially in summer. Lonely bridges, including one of the oldest on the river at Radcot and the wonderfully names Tadpole Bridge, are encountered. The walk passes close to the village of Kelmscott where William Morris lived. For those interested in visiting, the house and gardens are open to the public on Wednesdays and Saturdays between April and October. The meadow grasslands of Chimney Meadows should be looking their best in early summer. Your peace may be interrupted by military aircraft practising their manoeuvres overhead.

Transport options

Lechlade is served by buses between Fairford and Swindon, but this is remotest Thames and the staging points, Radcot Bridge after 6¼ miles (10 km) and Tadpole Bridge a further 4 miles (6.4 km), have no transport. Buses serve the villages to the north and south of the Thames and link Newbridge with Abingdon and Witney except on Sundays.

Things to look out for

1 Lechlade This small, prosperous town has a marketplace with several coaching inns, and the streets radiate out from it, their golden Cotswold stone mingling with the greys of Oxfordshire. The spire of St Lawrence, truly one of the great 'wool churches', draws the whole composition together. Indeed, Lechlade owes its location and its prosperity to having long been the highest point on the Thames that laden barges could reach. The riverside is still busy, but where once Cotswold stone and Gloucestershire cheeses were loaded up for London, it is now gleaming, white pleasure cruisers that congregate at the head of navigation. Unfortunately the peace of the place is disturbed by the traffic that thunders through the town, as it is on the junction of two main roads.

2 St John's Lock Here, in front of the lock house, you can pay your respects to Old Father Thames, reclining with symbols of commerce around him. He was first commissioned in 1854 for the grounds of Crystal Palace, then bought by one of the Thames Conservators and set beside the Thames Head spring (see page 10) to gaze at occasional visitors from a cage of railings. Doubtless he is happier here, watching the boats. St John's Bridge, beyond the lock, is Victorian, but earlier versions were administered by St John's Priory, established here in

1250. Nothing remains of the priory, but probably some of its stones were re-used in the nearby Trout Inn. See Locks and Weirs, page 17.

3 Pillboxes These concrete defences sitting quietly along this section of the river date back to the Second World War. They are slowly decaying, but at least one has been put to use as a nesting home for bats. In their tranquil settings it is difficult to believe that, in 1940, they formed a defence line along the river called Stop Line Red – a last desperate bid to keep invaders from reaching the Midlands. At that time, after the Dunkirk debacle, Britain was very vulnerable to invasion and morale was low. These pillboxes were designed to stop Rommel's panzer divisions in

their tracks, but were virtually obsolete as soon as they were built and only ever manned once in a false alarm!

4 Buscot village St Mary's Church in Buscot village dates from 1200 and has some rare stained-glass windows made by the 19th-century artist Edward Burne-Jones. Along with Buscot Park, a large neo-classical manor house and gardens, it forms part of the Buscot Estate. This is the family home of Lord Farringdon, but it is administered by the National Trust and open to the public between April and September. Well worth a visit, the house is full of art, including a Rembrandt, while the gardens feature a four seasons walled garden and a 'faux fall' – a sculpture that looks like a waterfall.

Lechlade Bridge, better known as Ha'penny Bridge, retains its little toll house.

5 Eaton Weir This was one of the last of the primitive flash-weirs on the Thames, and was taken up in 1936. A touch of sadness lingers at this location now: the Anchor Inn that stood on the far bank for many years was destroyed by fire some years ago in tragic circumstances, and no trace remains. The only building that survives today is the attractive little weir-keeper's cottage.

6 Kelmscott See box, page 56

7 Eaton Hastings Today Eaton Hastings consists of a scattering of houses around the church alongside the south bank of the river. In the past it was a much larger place, and it can almost be classified as a deserted medieval village. The most prominent building is St Michael's Church, parts of which date from the 11th century.

8 Radcot Bridge Parts of old Radcot Bridge date to the 12th century, a time when only the religious houses had building skills like this. The three Gothic arches are built of Taynton stone and ribbed beneath like a cathedral roof, and one parapet still carries the niche that once held a statue of the Virgin Mary. Radcot Bridge has had a dramatic history, in that it was badly damaged during a battle between Loyalists and Parliamentarians in 1387 and again later during the War of the Roses, before becoming an important toll bridge and commercial trade centre. However, the main river traffic was diverted along the other channel channel in 1787 with the building of the Thames–Severn Canal, leaving Radcot to age gently on a quiet backwater. See Bridges, page 19.

9 Rushey Lock and Weir One of the few surviving paddle-and-rymer weirs, this is a listed structure. Before the arrival of pound locks, a weir like this had to be opened by drawing out some of the paddles (you will see some stacked by the path) from between the rymers (heavier posts with handles). The river traffic passed through the gap as soon as the resulting 'flash' of water had subsided. Rushey Weir is due to be automated in 2013. See Locks and Weirs, page 17.

10 Tadpole Bridge This remote late-18th-century bridge, with its one large arch, delightful name and only a solitary inn for company, was built to carry the turnpike road to Bampton.

11 Chimney Meadow National Nature Reserve Chimney Meadow is a nationally important site for unimproved grassland. Consisting of six large wildflower meadows, it has large populations of adder's tongue fern, pepper saxifrage and meadow rue, and is a haven for butterflies and other wildlife. It is best visited in May and June for wild flowers and December to February for wintering birds.

12 Lost town of Shifford This very small place to the north of the river consists of a scattering of houses and a 19th-century chapel. It has been a tiny hamlet for many years but is reputed to be the location where King Alfred held a meeting of the English Parliament with 'many bishops, learned men, proud earls and awful knights'. They would not recognise it now.

Route description

Take time to explore **Lechlade ⏸**, then follow the towpath under an arch of Ha'penny Bridge, with two gates taking you into open meadowland, round bends of the river and through two more gates to **St John's Lock ⏹**. To avoid the 42 steps built into the Bloomers Hole footbridge ahead, an alternative route crosses St John's Bridge to turn right beyond the Trout Inn, then right again in 350 yards (320 metres) on a track through two gates and back to the Thames.

📖 *To visit the Trout Inn, turn left over the bridge and the pub is on the right-hand side.*

The route keeps to the old towpath, beneath the bridge arch, then through a gate into the meadows beyond. A footbridge crosses a broad side-stream, then the footbridge at Bloomers Hole **A** with a gate at each end takes you over the Thames. Turn downstream to follow the serpentine river – here fenced off and no short-cuts allowed. In the open meadows are **pillboxes ⏹**, some so eroded as to look like tiny medieval castles. Across the Thames stands **Buscot** Church **⏹**, and beside it the fine Old Parsonage of the Queen Anne period, part of the Buscot Estate. At Buscot Lock, go

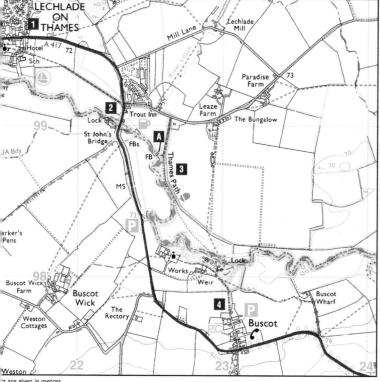

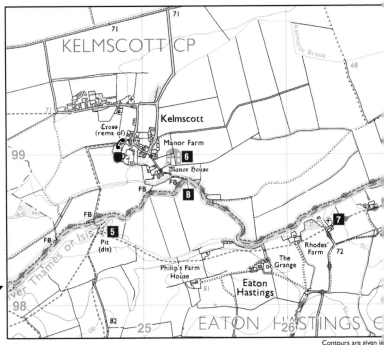

Contours are given i
The vertical interva

through the gate to walk ahead (not the stile on the left) and over the weir bridge to the lock.

🍵 *To visit the National Trust village of Buscot, with its quaint shop and tea room (limited winter opening times), cross the upper lock gates and the old weir on a path that passes the stone weir-keeper's cottage and the weir pool. Keep heading southwards on the track for ½ mile (0.8 km) to reach Buscot village, where the shop and tea room can be found on the left-hand side of the road.*

The Thames Path, however, continues on the grass along the lock edge, through a gate and along the water's edge before crossing a big concrete bridge over the main weir stream, and thus back to the riverside again. Around more meanders, in a grove of trees ahead, you come to

Eaton Weir 5, a pretty spot with a rustic bridge and a tiny cottage; but no weir. Stay on the same bank, squeeze past the footbridge and carry on, with the river still to your right. Soon, a footbridge and gate **B** lead you into a broad track.

Your route lies onward, but, to the left, the track will take you, in just a couple of minutes, to **Kelmscott Manor 6**, the serene Elizabethan house that William Morris fell in love with and made his country home for 25 years – see box, page 56.

To visit Kelmscott Manor, turn left here along the road and the house soon appears on your left. Keep ahead to visit the tiny village of Kelmscott. Bear left at the junction and ᗏ the Plough Inn will be found on the left.

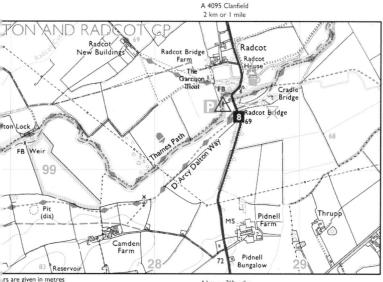

Keep on along the broad track by the Thames, then through a large kissing-gate into open meadows again through a gate by a pillbox. Soon, across the river, a lawn, a house or two and a glimpse of a simple church among the trees tell you that you are passing **Eaton Hastings 7**. Go through another large kissing-gate, then two further gates and in the next grove of trees is Grafton Lock, where you walk through the gate, along the lawn, between the flowerbeds and straight on towards Radcot. Out of season you may well pass through a temporary boatyard where the boats are in 'dry dock' on the edge of a field. Before reaching Radcot, the river divides, and while you follow the left-hand branch through a gate and over a wooden footbridge up to the road beside the narrow, much-scraped navigation bridge, you can see that the other branch flows under the far older **Radcot Bridge 8**.

Coming to the road, take great care of passing traffic as you cross the newer bridge, then turn down the steps and go through a gate to the river bank, and soon a bridge with a gate at each end takes you over the old Thames channel and then straight on.

📖 *To visit the Swan Hotel, Radcot, turn left on the bridge by the traffic lights and the pub is soon reached on the right-hand side of the road.*

Lonely Radcot Bridge, one of the oldest on the Thames.

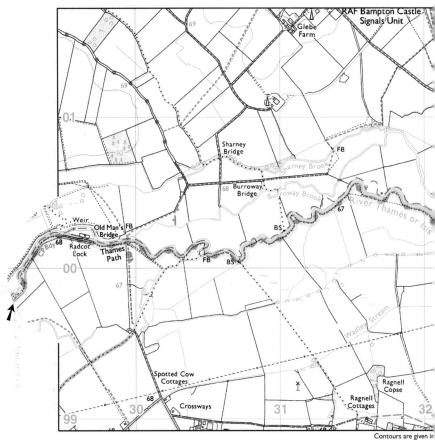

At Radcot Lock, take the grassy path past the lock itself, then walk briefly along the access drive before leaving it to return to the river bank. Past Old Man's Bridge, lonely in the fields, there are more meanders in the river; in fact, you can try guessing where the Thames will wander next. Continue ahead, crossing occasional footbridges over side-streams. At **Rushey Lock and Weir** 9, your way crosses the weir, then takes a gravel path across the garden past the charming stone lock cottage and over the lower lock gates to the road.

The lock access road follows the river now to **Tadpole Bridge** 10. The steps on the right take you up to the road, where you cross over, looking out for passing traffic, before dropping down to the towpath straight ahead.

📖 *To visit the Trout Inn, turn right on the bridge and the pub lies back from the road on the left-hand side.*

The path takes you via three large kissing-gates through open meadows, at the end of which is a gate a little way up from the river. Here the path is narrower

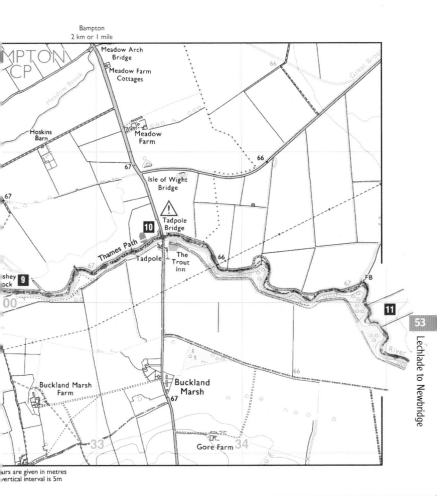

Bampton
2 km or 1 mile

Meadow Arch Bridge
Meadow Farm Cottages
MPTON CP
Hoskins Barn
Meadow Farm
Isle of Wight Bridge
67
67
⚠ Tadpole Bridge
10
Thames Path
Tadpole
The Trout Inn
66
67
FB
11
9
shey ock
00
67
River

Buckland Marsh Farm
Buckland Marsh
67
33
Gore Farm 34

66
66
66

Great Brook
Meadow Brook

urs are given in metres
vertical interval is 5m

and more enclosed, and can be slippery in the wet. Avenues of slender trees provide a useful guide to where the Thames runs, as you wend your way via a gate into **Chimney Meadow National Nature Reserve 11**, one of the largest areas of unimproved meadowland in England, rich in hay-meadow plants.

The Adonis Blue butterfly can be seen in the grasses of Chimney Meadows.

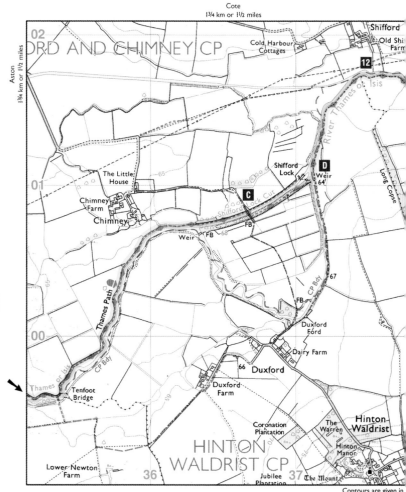

Cote
1¾ km or 1½ miles

Shifford
Old Shi
Farm

ORD AND CHIMNEY CP

Cold Harbour
Cottages

12

Aston
1¾ km or 1½ miles

River Thames or Isis

The Little
House

Shifford
Lock

D
Weir
64'

Long Copse

01

Chimney
Farm
Chimney

C

Shifford ock Cut

Weir FB

FB

Weir FB

Thames Path

FB
CP Bdy
67

Duxford
Ford

00

Dairy Farm

Thames or Isis

CP Bdy

66 Duxford

Thames
Tenfoot
Bridge

Duxford
Farm

Hinton
Waldrist

Coronation
Plantation

The
Warren

Hinton
Manor

HINTON
WALDRIST CP

Lower Newton
Farm

36

37 The Mount

Jubilee
Plantation

Contours are given in
The vertical interval

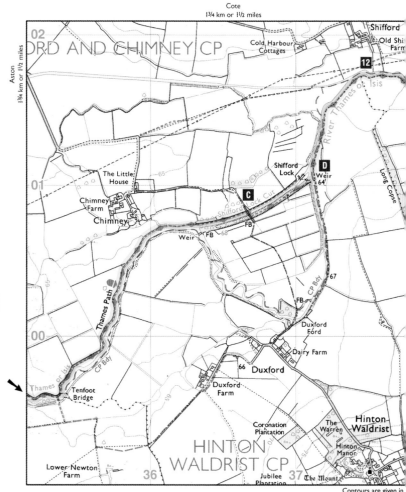

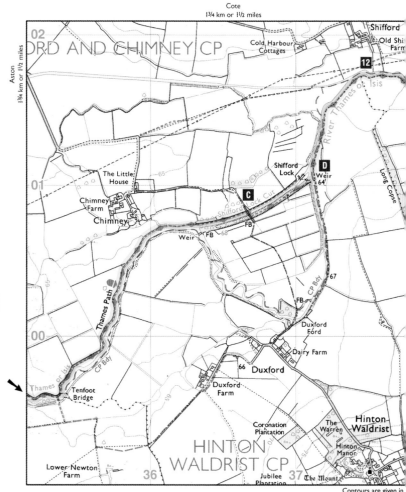

Your path keeps to the bank beside the river, taking you to Tenfoot Bridge. Like several other lonely footbridges on the upper Thames, Tenfoot is on the site of a flash-weir, taken up in 1870. Though the weir has gone, the right of way claimed by locals crossing over it has been preserved by a footbridge. The 'tenfoot' probably referred to the opening in the weir that let barges through.

Do not cross here, but keep on along the river bank. Soon you will see the distant buildings of Chimney Farm to your left, then across the river a weir that takes the old Thames channel looping away towards Duxford, still, as the name suggests, a genuine Thames ford. Now, as you pass through a large kissing-gate, you are following an artificial cut along a more enclosed woodland path, soon crossed by a wooden bridleway bridge **C**. Climb the steps and cross the bridge,

54

Lechlade to Newbridge

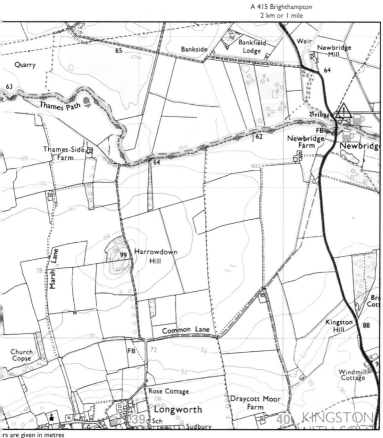

rs are given in metres
ertical interval is 5m

turning left in a few yards through a gate on to a path along an open green strip. Now the lock cut is to your left and, walking on beneath a fine, tall stand of poplar, you can hear the water surging over Shifford Weir. Just beyond it, bear right over a footbridge **D** and turn leftwards along the river bank, round the edge of a vast field. Just a meadow away, across the Thames, you can see a farm, a scattering of cottages and a tiny 19th-century chapel. This is **Shifford 12** where, unbelievably, there must have been a major town 1,000 years ago. After one more bend of the river and a wooded stretch beneath Harrowdown Hill, the path opens up and straightens.

To reach the village of Longworth and the Blue Boar Inn, take the footpath to the right which heads directly south over Harrowdown Hill.

You are now on the final run to Newbridge, keeping straight ahead and passing through several gates in the process. Go through one last gate, over a short footbridge and walk alongside the garden of the Maybush pub, up to the road. Turn left over the bridge, but take great care, as the road can be very busy and the traffic is controlled by lights.

Kelmscott Manor, William Morris's 'loveliest haunt of ancient peace'.

Kelmscott

William Morris, the famous 19th-century poet, craftsman, designer and socialist, fell in love with this country estate on the banks of the Thames and spent 25 years here. Born in Walthamstow in 1834, he was educated at Oxford, where he befriended Edward Burne-Jones, the artist who would become a major influence in the Pre-Raphaelite movement. Together with another friend, the architect Philip Webb, they formed the Arts and Crafts movement. It was through another friendship, with the poet and artist Dante Gabriel Rossetti, that Morris became such an influential figure in the decoration of houses and churches in the early 20th century.

Before his move to the country, he lived in the Red House at Bexleyheath, which was the first architectural commission by Philip Webb and was decorated by Morris. He later bought a London house on the Thames at Hammersmith, which walkers will pass much later, on the London leg of their Thames Path journey. Kelmscott Manor, deep in the countryside near the Thames, became Morris's country home in 1871. It is said that, on occasions, he would row his family and guests the 130 miles (209 km) from London house to country manor.

Morris chose Kelmscott for his home as he loved the 'organic nature' of this beautiful Elizabethan manor house, which seems to sit so perfectly in its surroundings. He described it as 'the loveliest haunt of ancient peace' and it remained a place of retreat and simple country living into his later years. Its grounds, with barns, dovecote, streams, meadow and formal gardens, were a constant source of inspiration for him, and the images he found here are reflected in his textile and wallpaper designs. He died in 1896 and is buried in the nearby churchyard of St George's Church, Kelmscott, under a simple, decorated, stone slab, the work of his friend Philip Webb.

The house today contains a wealth of Morris's works and possessions, and those of his contemporaries. Both house and gardens are owned by the Society of Antiquaries of London and are open to the public on Wednesdays and Saturdays from April to October.

Public transport

Newbridge (on route) 🚌 (not Sundays)
Taxis/minicabs: Lechlade, Carterton, Faringdon, Bampton and Southmoor

Refreshments and toilets

Lechlade St John's Lock (on route) 🍺 Trout Inn
Buscot (0.4 mile/0.6 km) 🍵 Buscot Park Tearoom (limited opening times)
Kelmscott (0.3 mile/0.5 km) 🍺 Plough Inn
Radcot (on route) 🍺 Swan Inn
Tadpole Bridge (on route) 🍺 Trout Inn
Longworth (1.2 miles/1.9 km) 🍺 Blue Boar
Newbridge (on route) 🍺 Maybush, Rose Revived
Food shops: Lechlade, Buscot (limited opening)
Public toilets: Lechlade, Lechlade St Johns Lock, Buscot, Grafton Lock, Radcot Lock, Rushey Lock, Shifford Lock

Accommodation

Buscot Wick (0.5 mile/0.8 km) Weston Farm
Kelmscott (0.3 mile/0.5 km) Manor Farm, Plough Inn
Radcot (on route) Swan Inn: campsite only
Faringdon (2.8 miles/4.5 km) wide selection – contact Visitor Information Centre
Clanfield (1.8 miles/2.4 km) Cotswold Plough Hotel
Bampton (2.2 miles/3.5 km) Coach House, Upham House, Wheelgate House
Tadpole Bridge (on route) Trout Inn
Rushey Lock (on route) campsite
Buckland (1.5 miles/2.4 km) Ashtree Farmhouse
Longworth (1.2 miles/1.9 km) Morlands, The Limes
Newbridge (on route) Rose Revived

The tiny village of Kelmscott, on the north bank of the Thames.

4 Newbridge to Oxford

via Bablock Hythe and Swinford Bridge
14 miles (22.5 km)

On this section the River Thames continues to grow slowly and more river craft can be seen negotiating the locks, especially in summer. Despite this, the route is still remote and barely a settlement is passed. Even the approach to Oxford itself is surprisingly rural, with lovely views of the famous dreaming spires across the vast expanse of Port Meadow. Thirsty walkers can be reassured that there are two famous and historic pubs towards Oxford, at Lower Wolvercote and Binsey. This section is a treat at any time of year, but in late spring the flood meadows are full of wild flowers and the autumn colours of Wytham Great Wood can be breathtaking.

Transport options

From Newbridge a 4-mile (6.4-km) walk brings you to Bablock Hythe, served by buses between Bampton and Oxford (except Sundays) and a further 3½ miles (5.6 km) to Swinford Bridge, where from nearby Eynsham and Farmoor there are good bus links every day into Oxford.

Things to look out for

1 Newbridge Try to savour this spot in the tranquillity of early morning, before the traffic has begun to rumble through. Then the glowing stone of the bridge is reflected in the still waters, the incredibly ancient arches caught in perfect mirror image. Newbridge is a 13th-century work, little altered and probably 'newer' than the bridge you passed at Radcot (pages 48 and 51) by 50 years or less. Its stone surely came from the Taynton quarries near Burford, rafted down the Windrush, which enters here. Indeed, this must once have been a busy wharf – the point where Taynton stone began its journey down the Thames to help build the Oxford colleges and even St Paul's Cathedral. Today there is just the bridge and, on either bank, the hostelries with their dreamily poetic names – Maybush and Rose Revived.

2 Bablock Hythe The Romans forded here, then there was a ferry crossing for perhaps 1,000 years. In the Second World War a chain-hauled vehicle ferry was kept busy, but today, even with an inn called The Ferryman nearby, you are unable to cross the river. Standing by the old ferry point, you can't help recalling Matthew Arnold's *Scholar Gipsy*, who 'oft was met crossing the stripling Thames at Bab-lock-hythe'. In his search for solitude, the Scholar Gipsy would not have approved of the chalet estate that mars this spot now.

3 Stanton Harcourt The thatched cottages, church, manor house and 17th-century parsonage of Stanton Harcourt are an impressive group. The church is outstanding for its Harcourt chapel, and the manor house equally so for the medieval great kitchen and nearby Pope's Tower.

4 Swinford Toll Bridge This is the first of the two remaining privately owned toll bridges on the Thames, the other being at Whitchurch, which you will encounter later on the walk. Swinford Bridge was built for the Earl of Abingdon around 1770 and is governed by its own Act of Parliament. The bridge is free to pedestrians, but it is a hectic job collecting the 5p tolls from every passing car on this busy road. See Bridges, page 19.

5 Eynsham A Bronze Age ditch and Roman remains are evidence of the age of human habitation at Eynsham, which developed as a settlement near to Swinford because it was just above the floodplain and at a location where it was easy to ford the river. Eynsham once had one of the most important abbeys in the country, but it fell into ruins between 1538 and 1657 during the dissolution of the monasteries under Henry VIII. An Abbey Heritage Trail has been established and the church of St Leonard's is well worth a visit.

6 River Evenlode A tributary of the Thames, the Evenlode rises in the Cotswolds near Moreton-in-Marsh, passing close to Stow-on-the-Wold and Charlbury before entering the north bank of the Thames near Wytham Great Wood. Hilaire Belloc referred to the River Evenlode in some of his poetry.

7 Godstow Abbey All that remains here is a walled enclosure with, in one corner, the shell of a 16th-century chapel. Godstow Abbey was founded in 1139 and became a kind of finishing school for daughters of the nobility. It has romantic associations

with Rosamund de Clifford, who was a mistress of Henry II. Rosamund was a favoured pupil, and after a mysterious death was brought back here for burial. Ironically, the best-surviving fragment of her abbey is the lovely old Trout Inn over the bridge, first built in 1138 as its hospice.

8 Port Meadow This vast area of ancient grazing land has never been ploughed and has remained unchanged since William the Conqueror presented it to the burgesses of Oxford as free common in return for helping William defend his kingdom from the marauding Danes. Often flooded in winter, it is grazed by cattle and horses and is a wonderful recreational asset to the city of Oxford.

The Thames wends its way past the Trout Inn, Godstow, to the vast expanse of Port Meadow.

Route description

Your walk starts out along the riverside terrace of 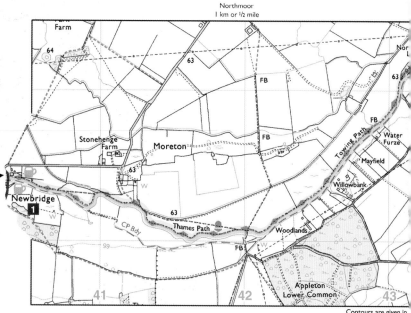 the Rose Revived, which is reached by a garden gate. Look back at ancient **Newbridge 1** as it copes with the demands of modern traffic levels. Following the water's edge over the lawn, you will find the towpath again, initially tight to the river bank, then through a gate into open meadows, ready to take you round more amiable meanders of the Thames. Pass over a concrete bridge and a short section of permissive path and enter a large field – managed by Natural England to encourage ground-nesting birds – through a large kissing-gate. Soon you come to another lonely bridge, Hart's Weir Footbridge, which links one remote meadow with another in puzzling fashion. Like others you have passed, this crossing preserves the right of way over an early Thames weir, long since taken up.

Now the river is beginning its great loop around the high ground of Cumnor and Wytham Hill. On the right day, this stretch can be sheer joy. Forget about route-finding and just stride out over the springy turf of these open meadows, through occasional gates, while the Thames unfolds an endless variety of compositions worthy of the brushes of a Constable.

After crossing a side-stream by footbridge you arrive at Northmoor Lock, where you go through the gate and over the grass to pass by the lockside and out again into open meadows. For safety and greater efficiency, the old paddle-and-rymer

Contours are given in
The vertical interval

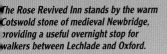

The Rose Revived Inn stands by the warm Cotswold stone of medieval Newbridge, providing a useful overnight stop for walkers between Lechlade and Oxford.

weir here is due to be automated by the Environment Agency during 2012/13. See Locks and Weirs, page 17.

📖 *A footpath to the left leads to the village of Northmoor and the Red Lion pub 1 mile (1.6 km) across the fields.*

Pass under the power lines and, after another mile or so of delightful riverside path, the gleam of white river craft and the hint of caravans through the trees ahead tell you that you are approaching **Bablock Hythe** 2, the best known of all the Thames crossings.

Here you leave the river for a while. From the Ferryman Inn turn up the approach lane, with the chalet estate to your right, keeping straight ahead at a junction along the Stanton Harcourt road.

At the ferry junction, buses run to Bampton and Oxford except on Sundays.

After another 300 yards (275 metres), by a passing place, go through a gate on the right on to a bridleway A. Through several more gates, the bridleway follows the left-hand field boundary, with views opening out on to the high ground of Wytham Great Wood over to the right. The metalled track you finally enter comes down from **Stanton Harcourt** 3, a village well deserving a visit, if you have the time.

Turn left up the track for 0.9 miles (1.4 km) to reach the attractive thatched village of Stanton Harcourt and the Harcourt Arms.

The Thames Path turns right along the track, back towards the river. When it ends, at a gate B, go through the kissing-gate alongside and turn left to walk near to the field boundary on your left. Through a gate into the next field, your way bears right along a faint track over the grass towards an exit point, visible in the far corner.

Go right through a gate over a concrete bridge, then go left through a further kissing-gate and into another meadow. Using the distant hill as the point to aim for, cross through the centre of the meadow until you again meet the Thames at the bottom. Two paths come to the river bank at this spot C, where, until the 1930s, a footbridge crossed at the site of another ancient weir, Skinner's Weir. No trace remains today, so bear left and follow the bank through a gate, leaving it briefly to skirt

Bluebells in the Oxford University Arboretum at Stanton Harcourt

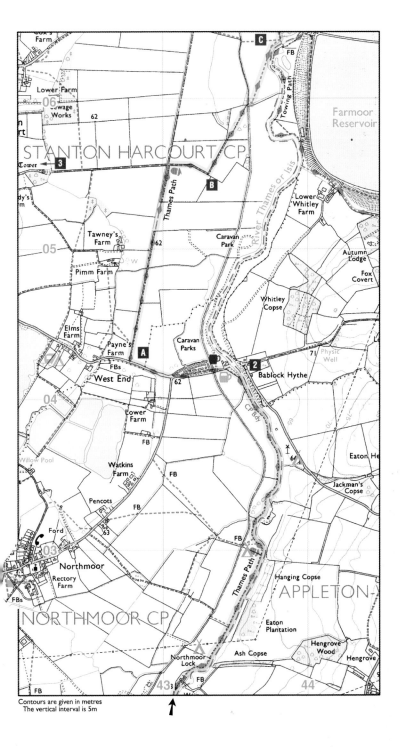

Contours are given in metres
The vertical interval is 5m

around a marvellously verdant backwater. Through a kissing-gate, you can see your path cutting off a river loop and heading directly across the grass via another kissing-gate to Pinkhill Weir. Cross the weir bridge, then take a path over the grass of the lock island to cross over the upper gates of the lock. Go through a gate on the right,

then turn left over the gravel outside the lock enclosure to reach the towpath again.

At the next bend, beyond a footbridge, the old towpath has been eroded away and lost, so a short diversion away from the river is necessary. Take the enclosed path up to the road, turn left and, after 250 yards (230 metres), turn left again

Contours are given in metres
The vertical interval is 5m

2 km or 1 mile
B 4017 Cumnor

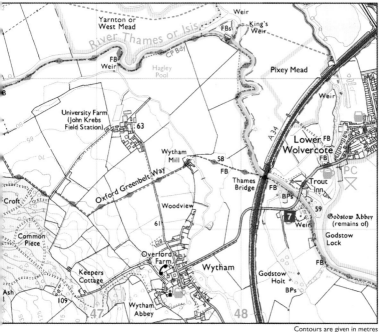

Contours are given in metres
The vertical interval is 5m

down the drive to Oxford Cruisers **D**. Walk through the boatyard to bear right to a gate on to the towpath again. More twists and loops lead via a short but high wooden footbridge on to the elegant arches of **Swinford Bridge 4**. Your path goes under one of the arches and keeps ahead on the river bank.

🚌 🚉 *For Eynsham, the Talbot Inn and buses to Oxford, go up steps to the road and cross Swinford Bridge. The village of **Eynsham 5** is well worth a visit.*

Immediately beyond Swinford Bridge is Eynsham Lock, where a modest path leads on over a footbridge and past the water works to where Wytham Great Wood comes steeply down to the water's edge. This fine 600-acre (243-hectare) wood, a wildlife haven, was bequeathed to Oxford University in the 1940s by Colonel Raymond ffennell, who owned the Wytham Estate. The path is a delight, as it winds through the woodland by the river. Back through a gate and in open pasture again, the Cotswold stream with the delectable name of **Evenlode 6** slips modestly into the Thames. Cross a weir by a large concrete footbridge and through a gate; the path continues ahead.

Pass straight through King's Lock and a large kissing-gate to continue onwards by the river around a couple of tight bends. The rumble of traffic indicates that a major road is ahead and you soon go under the Oxford bypass bridge. You pass a sadly damaged iron boundary marker of 1886 with the ox of Oxford on top, and then arrive at Godstow.

To the left, you can see the old channel flowing under the ancient two-arch bridge, which has, like Radcot Bridge (pages 48 and 51), been preserved by diverting the navigation to a new channel. Your path goes up to the road and straight across through two gates into the meadow, where you pass by all that remains of **Godstow Abbey** 7.

📖 To visit the historic Trout Inn 📖 at Lower Wolvercote, popularised by Lewis Carroll and Inspector Morse, turn left over the bridge and the pub can be found immediately on your right.

The track past the abbey leads to Godstow Lock, where you continue ahead through two gates with the vast,

open grazing of **Port Meadow** 8 across the river. As the river curves, the famous skyline of Oxford opens up across the meadow. This part of the river is a wonderful stretch with constantly changing views.

📖 A footpath soon leads off to the right, taking you the short distance to the historic, thatched Perch pub at Binsey, which also has many literary associations.

The little line of cottages of Binsey stays hidden until you near the end of their open green. Look back for a moment here, to see the tiny hamlet, tucked beneath the backdrop of Wytham

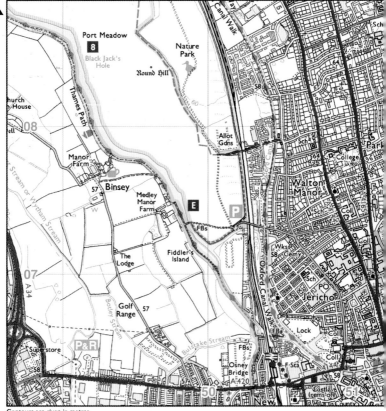

Contours are given in metres
The vertical interval is 5m

Woods. Then carry on through a gate past Bossom's Boatyard to cross Medley footbridge **E** and proceed along the other bank.

Soon a footbridge to your left crosses into Port Meadow, but your path continues over the bridge ahead, along a causeway bank, the Thames to the right, a wetlands strip to the left – a surprisingly lush and rural entry into Oxford. Finally, cross by footbridge over a feeder waterway signposted to the Oxford Canal, and walk past cottage gardens up to the road at Osney Bridge.

≥ ⬛⟐ *Oxford station is along the road to your left. Although the centre of Oxford is best reached from Folly Bridge further along the Thames Path, you can also get to the city centre along this road.*

For a walk around Oxford, see page 76.

Public transport
Bablock Hythe 🚌 (not Sundays)
Eynsham (0.9 mile/1.4 km) 🚌
Taxis/minicabs: Southmoor, Oxford

Refreshments and toilets
Northmoor (1 mile/1.6 km) ⬛ Red Lion
Bablock Hythe (on route) ⬛ Ferryman Inn
Stanton Harcourt (0.9 mile/1.4 km) ⬛ Harcourt Arms
Eynsham (0.9 mile/1.4 km) ⬛ Talbot Inn
Lower Wolvercote (0.1 mile/0.2 km) ⬛ Trout Inn
Binsey (0.2 mile/0.3 km) ⬛ The Perch
Oxford (on route) ⬛⟐ wide selection
Food shops: Eynsham, Oxford
Public toilets: Northmoor Lock, Pinkhill Lock, Eynsham Lock, Wolvercote, Oxford

Accommodation
Standlake (1 mile/1.6 km) The Cottage, Amberley House, Lincoln Farm Park Campsite, Hardwick Parks Campsite
Kingston Bagpuize/Southmoor (2.2 miles/3.5 km) Fallowfields Country House Hotel
Northmoor (1 mile/1.6 km) Rectory Farm
Bablock Hythe (on route) Ferryman
Pinkhill Lock (on route) campsite
Eynsham Lock (on route) campsite
Eynsham (0.9 miles/1.5 km) Talbot Inn, White Hart
Oxford (on route) wide selection – contact Visitor Information Centre

5 Oxford to Abingdon

via Sandford-on-Thames
9¾ miles (15.6 km)

This short section of the Thames Path allows some time to explore Oxford, although you will need at least a day to do it any justice. (For a walk highlighting the best of the city's many attractions, see page 76.) Beyond the surprisingly rural suburbs of Oxford and the brief intrusion of the Oxford Bypass, you will again pass through quiet and empty countryside with Sandford-on-Thames as the only settlement of any size between Oxford and Abingdon. After separating into channels through Oxford, the river now rejoins and has grown in size as it heads southwards on a long, gentle curve towards Abingdon. You will pass Sandford Lock, the largest lock on the Thames, and its associated weir, known as the Sandford Lasher, which has claimed many lives. The historic riverside town of Abingdon is a fitting end to this section.

Transport options

From Osney Bridge a 6-mile (9.7-km) walk brings you to Lower Radley, where there are nearby railway connections at Radley Station. Abingdon has frequent bus services to Oxford and to Didcot Parkway railway stations.

Things to look out for

1 Folly Bridge Once known as Grandpont, its better-known name comes from an idiosyncratic building that once stood over the north end of an earlier bridge at this spot. In the form of an archway with a tower on top, it was used as an observatory by the 13th-century friar Roger Bacon and became known as 'Friar Bacon's Study'. It was not pulled down until 1779. The Victorian house by today's bridge, with its castellated skyline and assortment of statues in niches, keeps the 'folly' theme intact.

2 Iffley Church St Mary's Church, dating from the 12th century, is richly decorated in Romanesque style with fantastic beasts and zig-zag stonework inside and out. You can reach it by the path over the rustic footbridge, then by the lock and weirs, and finally by climbing the little lane up from the river and turning right. On the way, you may notice a plaque on the site of the first pound lock on the Thames, and then a millstone – all that remains of Iffley Mill.

3 Sandford-on-Thames This small village is mentioned in the Domesday Book with a history of farming, fishing and milling. Paper-milling continued until as recently as 1982. The mill cottages remain unchanged and the mill race still runs. The river flows impressively here through the large weir, which has sadly taken many lives through drowning (see Locks and Weirs, page 17). There was a ferry here as early as the 13th century and, just beyond the lock, a stone mounting block is preserved from those days.

4 **Nuneham House** A large Palladian villa which was owned by Lord Harcourt, Nuneham House, overlooks the river valley from the eastern side of the Thames. The original house dates from 1756 and has been altered and added to several times, but the landscaping potential of the site seems to have been the big attraction. Lord Harcourt even had a village moved to give the famous Capability Brown full scope to beautify his grounds. Little of the landscaping survived the Second World War, but as you walk past you will see, prominent on its hill, the Jacobean Carfax Conduit, once a feature of Oxford's water supply, now serving simply as a garden ornament.

5 **Swift Ditch** This ancient and overgrown channel, marked as Back Water on maps, cuts off a large loop in the river. There is conjecture that this was once the main route, but it was more likely to have been dug by monks of Abingdon Abbey around 1052 to improve the course of the river. When Abingdon Lock opened in 1790, this channel fell into disuse.

The Thames from Oxford's Folly Bridge.

Route description

You will see little of dreaming spires from the Thames Path as it skirts around Oxford's edge. Indeed, unless you succumb to the urge to break off and explore, your encounter with the city will be pleasantly green and surprisingly brief. From Osney Bridge, cross the river and set off on the south bank via a girder bridge over a tributary stream, then along the grass in front of a charming terrace of riverside cottages on East Street.

Beyond the Punter Inn, the path leaves the road to cross the weir streams of Osney Lock, then passes the lock itself, with an old mill being developed beyond. This reminds us that, by repute, the earlier main channel of the Thames ran under Hythe Bridge, nearer the city centre, until the monks of now-vanished Osney Abbey directed it this way to work their mill.

Beyond the lock, the path is mercifully screened from nearby industry by

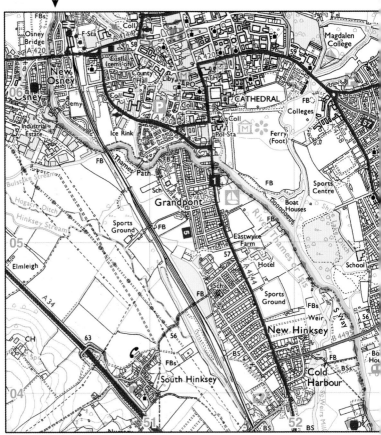

Contours are given in metres
The vertical interval is 5m

A narrowboat makes its way gently upstream south of Oxford.

foliage. On the far side of the railway bridge, the path continues along the riverside, but here you may be tempted to sample the unexpected views from Grandpont Nature Reserve on your right. It was created on the site of Oxford's gasworks. By the river you pass the modern ice rink and a handsome modern college residence, then, beyond Jubilee Terrace, your path curves with the Thames and climbs up to the road on **Folly Bridge 1**.

To explore Oxford city centre and to follow the walking tour described on page 76, turn left across the bridge.

The Thames Path keeps ahead to cross the road via the pedestrian lights then drops down to the river again. Once across, take two footbridges across side-streams and pass the traditional home of Salter Bros steamers on your left, then the tree-lined banks of Christ Church Meadow across the river. This is a rowing reach, and once the bank would have been lined with ornate college barges serving the double duty of clubhouses and grandstands. Alas, they have gone, either rotted away or converted to humbler uses. There is a row of boathouses on the far bank and one new and impressive University College boathouse to pass on our bank. Through the trees, you can glimpse a little of the Oxford skyline: a part of Merton College, the dome of the Radcliffe Camera – even a spire or two.

Cross two further footbridges and now you are walking through open fields with Oxford left behind; indeed, beyond the next road bridge you come to Iffley Meadows, 82 acres (33 hectares) of ancient watermeadow, where regular winter flooding enriches the clay soil with silt. The drooping purple heads of the rare snake's-head fritillary can be seen here in late April. Surrounded by meadow land, the Isis Farmhouse here depends largely on river trade – the bars are full of oars, skiffs and photos of stiffly posed rowing crews.

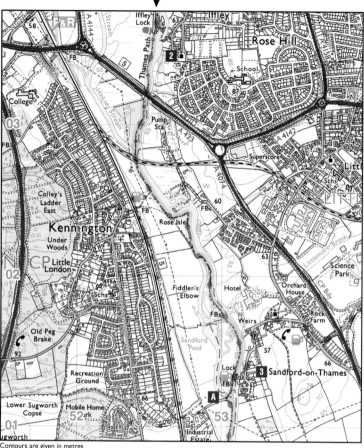

Contours are given in metres
The vertical interval is 5m

Then comes Iffley Lock, and over the trees, on the far bank, can be seen the sturdy tower of the superb Norman **Iffley Church** 2.

Continue ahead along this stretch of towpath, which is popular with cyclists and joggers, through a large kissing-gate and under a road bridge carrying the seemingly endless traffic on the Oxford ring road. A substantial footbridge takes you over the Hinksey Stream, then pass under a railway bridge into open meadows owned by

the Oxford Preservation Society and on towards **Sandford-on-Thames** 3, through a gate in some nicely stylised railings. A steel footbridge with a gate at one end crosses the weir stream, almost as broad as the Thames itself, and soon you hear turbulent water to your right. The lock up ahead has the greatest fall of water on the Thames, and the water thunders over the enormous weir known as the Sandford Lasher. Impressive and sometimes lethal, for the Lasher has claimed several lives; a memorial column stands on the weir as a reminder.

The Victorian mill that once stood by the lock has been replaced by housing, but the colourful little group of cottages across the lock is still attractive.

🍺 *Thirsty walkers will be relieved to know that they can reach the King's Arms by crossing the lower lock gates and the former mill stream. If passing through on a Saturday morning, you will find a weekly market and café held here.*

Walk ahead past the lock over a bridge and turn left along a narrow strip of car park, where you will find the towpath continuing at the end **A**.

A lush, wild stretch follows, with low hills rising across the river and good farmland on your side. Pass under the power lines on the narrow path, which can be slippery in the wet. Eventually the path opens out to give better views and you come, via a large kissing-gate, to the boathouses of Radley College, a public school with a strong rowing tradition. Cross the slipway to the boathouse by footbridge and keep on by the Thames.

🚉 🍺 *For Radley station or the Bowyer Arms, take the tree-lined lane on the right just beyond the college buildings, and turn right at a T-junction. Then turn immediately left to follow the lane towards Radley, where the station and the pub can be found to the left.*

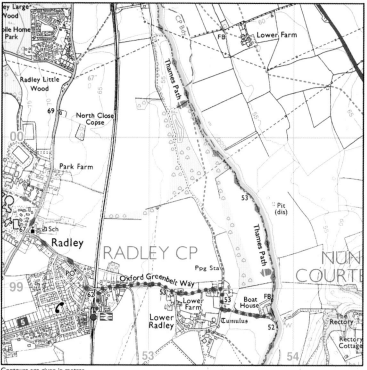

Contours are given in metres
The vertical interval is 5m

Beyond the boathouses, **Nuneham House** stands on the rise across the river. Keep by the Thames, crossing a short footbridge, more open meadowland and two short enclosed belts of woodland to reach the lawns of a riverside house. Further open meadows lead towards a railway bridge. Beyond comes a wild area of high grasses and scrubland left over from gravel workings, with paths heading off in several directions. Resist temptation, and follow the river on the narrow path past locally planted woodland. As you pass the second of two picnic sites you will see a weir across the Thames – one of the overgrown entries into the **Swift Ditch** (Back Water on the map), a morsel of Thames history that you will meet again soon.

Beyond the woodland planting, your path skirts around a verdant inlet, a wildlife haven with several viewing points for enjoying a watery scene of reeds and bulrushes. Back with the Thames again, cross a footbridge and take the path with just a ditch between you and the river bank. At a crossing path, turn left and go over another lush channel, the Abbey Stream, by a wooden footbridge, then turn left by its bank on the path to Abingdon Weir. Cross the weir, take the fenced path and cross the lower lock gates, then go right through a gate on to the towpath again; ahead are Abingdon and the spire of St Helen's – a classic Thames view.

As you walk through the arch of Abingdon Bridge, take a look back: you will see that it is far longer than you imagined – truly a causeway with many arches (see Bridges, page 19).

To explore Abingdon, go up the steps on either side of the bridge and walk up Bridge Street to the Market Place.

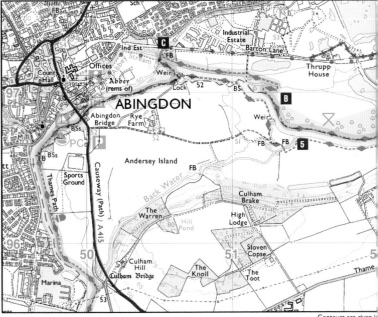

Contours are given in
The vertical interval

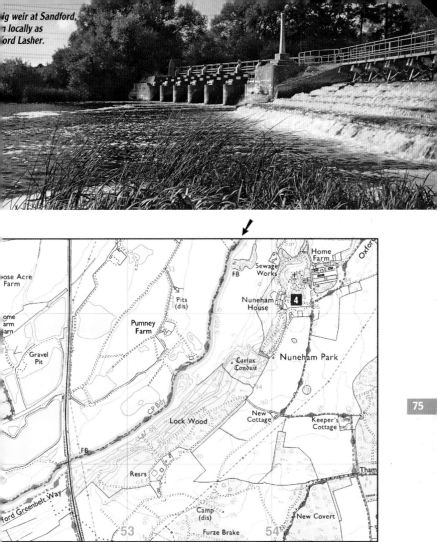

The big weir at Sandford, known locally as Sandford Lasher.

rs are given in metres
ertical interval is 5m

Public transport

Radley (0.9 mile/1.4 km) ≷
Abingdon (on route) 🚌
Taxis/minicabs: Oxford, Abingdon

Refreshments and toilets

Iffley Lock (on route) 🍴🍺 Isis
Farmhouse (limited opening times)
Sandford-on-Thames (on route) 🍴
King's Arms
Radley (0.9 mile/1.4 km) 🍴 Bowyer Arms

Abingdon (on route) 🍴🍺 wide
selection
Food shops: Radley, Abingdon
Public toilets: Oxford, Abingdon Lock,
Abingdon

Accommodation

Sandford-on-Thames (on route) Oxford
Thames Four Pillars
Abingdon (on route) wide selection –
contact Visitor Information Centre

A Circular Walk around Oxford

Starts and finishes at Folly Bridge
Total distance: 6 miles (9.6 km)

Please note that the walk passes through city and university parks where opening and closing times can vary throughout the year. For information about parks, visiting the colleges and other useful information, see page 165.

Coming up from the River Thames, turn left across Folly Bridge towards the city centre. Just beyond the Head of the River pub, turn right down an unnamed alleyway with signs for boat hire. Turn right at the end and continue round the back of the pub and over a small wooden footbridge. Beyond the bridge a high metal kissing-gate allows access into the university grounds of Christ Church Meadow (gate closes at 5pm). Turn right and then left on a woodchip path through the trees and over grass to meet a broad track. Turn left and follow the track towards the imposing **Christ Church College** buildings ahead.

At a T-junction in front of the college building your path meets a wider track known as Broad Walk. Turn right on to Broad Walk and then first left on to another path known as Dead Man's Walk. This name comes from the fact that Jewish funeral processions used to pass this way from the synagogue to the burial grounds. Follow the path, with the playing fields of Merton College on your right and the attractive buildings first of Christ Church and then of **Merton College** to your left.

Look out for the plaque in the wall marking the location of a very early balloon ascent by a James Sadler in 1784. Once you have passed the Merton buildings on your left, turn left to exit Christ Church Meadow through another very tall but narrow metal kissing-gate. Keep ahead into Rose Lane, following it to the High Street, which is lined with many grand buildings.

Turn left along the High Street and cross the road at the pedestrian lights on the junction of Longwall Street. Keep ahead in the same direction, passing the Oxford University Examination Schools and **University College** on the left, and **Queen's** and **All Souls Colleges** on your right.

Just before the magnificent and ornate parish church of **St Mary the Virgin**, turn

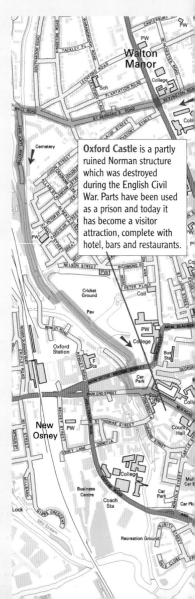

Oxford Castle is a partly ruined Norman structure which was destroyed during the English Civil War. Parts have been used as a prison and today it has become a visitor attraction, complete with hotel, bars and restaurants.

right into Catte Street. Beware of cyclists along this vehicle-free stretch of road before it opens out into Radcliffe Square, which is dominated by the round building of the **Radcliffe Camera**. Continue up Catte Street, which now has road traffic, and the building directly to the north of the Radcliffe Camera houses the world-famous **Bodleian Library.**

Oxford's main Tourist Information Centre is just round the corner from here in Broad Street, but having passed All Souls College to the right, turn next right into New College Lane, passing beneath the **Bridge of Sighs** – this copy of the famous Venetian bridge links two quads within Hertford College. (Note the tiny alleyway to your left – St Helen's Passage – which leads to the Turf Tavern pub,

The Bodleian Library is the main research library for Oxford University and one of the oldest libraries in Europe. Built in the 14th century it is named after Sir Thomas Bodley, who greatly expanded the library in the 1600s. It is the second biggest library in Britain after the British Library.

The Radcliffe Camera, a round building with a lofty tower, was built by James Gibbs between 1737 and 1749 and funded by the famous physicist John Radcliffe. It is a reading room for college undergraduates.

Magdalen College, founded in 1458, is one of the most beautiful and, with its prominent location by the Cherwell, one of the most visited of the Oxford colleges.

Christ Church is one of the largest of the Oxford colleges and is also uniquely the Cathedral Church of the diocese of Oxford. It has produced a long list of British prime ministers and the buildings have featured in many films.

Merton College was founded in 1264 by Walter de Merton, Lord Chancellor to Henry III, and has laid claim to being the oldest of the Oxford colleges. It boasts the world's oldest continually functioning academic library.

A Circular Walk around Oxford

made famous by Inspector Morse.) You now follow this wonderfully atmospheric, narrow road which passes the house of the famous astronomer Edmund Halley as it winds around the ancient walls of old colleges. The road turns into Queen's Lane as you pass the entrance to **New College** – which, despite its name, is one of Oxford's oldest colleges and has a strong choral tradition – before arriving back at the bustling High Street.

Here turn left and briefly retrace your steps before continuing on to follow the High Street past **Magdalen College** with the Oxford University Botanic Garden, the oldest in the country, across the road.

Cross the **River Cherwell** at Magdalen Bridge, from which students traditionally jumped into the river as part of the May Morning celebrations; recent lower water levels, however, have rendered this a dangerous pastime. When you reach a major road junction known as The Plain keep left into St Clement's Street. Ignore the first turning left into York Place but take the

Christ Church

next turning left towards St Clement's car park (*public toilets*) and carry on through into the Angel and Greyhound Meadow over a small footbridge at the bottom end of the car park. This meadow takes its name from two old coaching inns on the High Street where the grass was used as horse pasture. Turn right on the meadow, keeping the channel of the Cherwell on your right. Nearing trees, turn left and then right through a gap. When you notice a children's play area over on your left, head to the right to cross the river again by another footbridge which takes you into Bath Street. Turn immediately to the left along the surfaced path by the river in front of some houses.

This leads you through to the end of Cave Street. Walk up Cave Street a short distance before turning left down a narrow alleyway called Dudley Gardens. Follow this alley to the left and right along the side of the river to reach Cherwell Street. Turn right up Cherwell Street to emerge at a busy road junction.

Cross Marston Road to your left at the traffic lights and enter Headington Hill Park (opening hours vary but are usually 8am to dusk daily) just opposite through the gates. Walk through the park on the obvious surfaced path and turn left near another park entrance. Keep ahead until a newly built mosque appears down the hill to your left. Turn left down a gravel path towards the mosque to leave the park through a large metal gate. This brings you out on to Marston Road again, which you cross with care to go right and first left down a private road, King's Mill Lane, which is also a public footpath to the University Parks.

You pass Magdalen College playing field and Kings Mill (a watermill was recorded here in the Domesday Book) to enter **Oxford University Parks** (generally open at 7.45am daily, but closed 24/25 December and 1 January; see page 165). Keep ahead on a delightful surfaced path that follows a narrow ribbon of land between two channels of the Cherwell – this is the Mesopotamia Walk (from the Greek meaning 'between the rivers'), which was laid out in 1865.

Keep ahead with the river on your right until you reach a footbridge. Cross this, turning right through the gate at the end, and walk a short distance to go through a large iron

kissing-gate. Cross the concrete cycle path and turn left through the gate opposite to walk parallel to the cycle path for a short distance before joining it. Go over a bridge and right through another large iron kissing-gate into more Oxford University parkland. Merge with a larger track and keep ahead, with the river bank on your right. Ignoring the elegant footbridge – known as the Rainbow Bridge because of its shape – over the River Cherwell, keep to the track that circles around a large pond and heads off to the left away from the river. Remain on this main path, passing **Lady Margaret Hall** on the right and The Parks cricket ground on the left. Lady Margaret Hall was founded as the first women-only college in 1878, but has been co-educational since 1979. Here is the only first class cricket venue in the country where spectators don't have to pay. There are many fine trees to admire in the park, including seven giant sequoias and a Japanese pagoda tree.

Leave the park through North Lodge on to Parks Road, with the vast Science Park building looming nearby. Cross Norham Gardens and the very busy Banbury Road at a pelican crossing and turn right towards the theological college of Wycliffe Hall on the opposite side of the road. Take the first left into Bevington Road, passing the buildings of **St Anne's College**, which was women-only too and has also been co-educational since 1979. At the next road crossing keep ahead across Woodstock Road and into St Bernard's Road. At the next junction go half-right into Walton Well Road, which soon crosses over the **Oxford Canal**. Beyond the bridge, turn left into William Lucy Way, named after a 19th-century iron-foundry owner, and head immediately down the path on your left to the canal side. At the bottom of the slope keep ahead along the towpath. You are now close to the start of the attractive Oxford Canal Walk which extends for 82½ miles (132 km) from Oxford all the way to Coventry.

The towpath makes for pleasant walking and the banks of the canal are lined with colourful narrowboats. Keep on the towpath to arrive at Isis Lock with a pair of pedestrian bridges facing you. Take the left-hand bridge to continue for a short distance along a path between the canal and the river. The Oxford Canal abruptly stops just short of Hythe Bridge, but you continue ahead up to the road and turn right. Almost immediately cross at the pedestrian lights and turn left and down the steps of Fisher Row, now with the river on your left. At the next bridge go up the steps and turn left along Park End Road. Keep ahead into New Road, passing Nuffield College on your left and **Oxford Castle** to your right.

Keep ahead into Bonn Square and turn right into St Ebbe's Street just before the shopping area. Turn left into Pembroke Street to pass the buildings of **Pembroke College**, which was founded in 1624.

Pembroke Street meets St Aldate's Street at the end, so turn right to pass the imposing tower and buildings of Christ Church College towards Folly Bridge and the end of the walk.

6 Abingdon to Wallingford

via Clifton Hampden, Little Wittenham and Shillingford
13½ miles (21.7 km)

This scenically rewarding and varied section both starts and finishes in very attractive and historic riverside towns. Abingdon and Wallingford merit time to explore their fascinating back streets and old buildings. The route is dominated by great loops in the river and fascinating small settlements along the way. Two particular highlights are the wonderful juxtaposition of Clifton Hampden Bridge with the nearby church, and the varied landscapes around Little Wittenham. The springy turf and the long, slow loop of the river from Clifton Hampden Bridge to Day's Lock make exhilarating walking. Apart from a short section of road-walking near Shillingford, this is magnificent towpath walking at its best. Try to allow time to visit the ancient abbey of Dorchester.

Transport options

Culham, after 2¼ miles (3.5 km), has a railway station but services are infrequent and it is some distance from the river. Clifton Hampden, after another 3 miles (4.8 km), and Dorchester, near Day's Lock 2¾ miles (4.4 km) further on, are served by buses between Abingdon and Wallingford. Wallingford has good bus connections with Reading.

Things to look out for

1 Abingdon See box, page 82.

2 Culham This ancient hamlet is dominated by the Manor House, partly rebuilt in the 17th century on the base of what was originally a 15th-century grange of Abingdon Abbey. The whole ensemble of the Manor House, church, pub and cottages around a little green makes a perfect entity, charming to behold across the fields. An interesting feature is the gabled dovecote, which is big enough for 4,000 nesting places.

3 Sutton Courtenay This attractive village has a long history. The original settlement on this site dates from the 5th and 6th centuries and in the 1920s it became the first Anglo-Saxon village to be discovered by archaeologists. The

church of All Saints has carved Crusader crosses on a doorway in the 12th-century tower. In the churchyard are the graves of Herbert Asquith, Prime Minister from 1908–16; Eric Arthur Blair, otherwise known as George Orwell, the author of *Animal Farm* and *1984*; and David Astor, the newspaper publisher.

The village is famous for having three very historic domestic buildings. These are Sutton Courtenay Manor House, which has royal connections dating back to the 11th century. Matilda, the queen of Henry I, lived here and her daughter, the Empress Matilda, was probably born in this house. Most of the manor, though, dates from the 14th and 16th centuries. The other interesting buildings are the 13th-century rectory house, which is now called Sutton Courtenay Abbey, and a Norman hall dating from 1192, the oldest building in the village.

4 Appleford Church With its unusually fat spire, the parish church of St Peter and St Paul at Appleford is a landmark across the river bank towards Didcot. Parts of the church date to the 12th century, but changes, including the redesigned spire, were carried out in the Victorian era.

5 Clifton Hampden Thanks mainly to the great architect Sir George Gilbert Scott, Clifton Hampden is today an attractive hamlet of thatched cottages, church and bridge. Scott designed the bridge that replaced the ferry in 1864, and restored the little church on its viewpoint bluff, which can be reached by a long flight of steps. The thatched pub, the Barley Mow, one of the most famous on the Thames, dates from 1352 and was built using the traditional 'cruck' construction. As Jerome K. Jerome pointed out in *Three Men in a Boat*, the doors are low too: 'Duck or grouse', as the sign over the entrance says.

6 Little Wittenham A small hamlet located close to Day's Lock, Little Wittenham can be reached by crossing the footbridge here, which has won fame as the location for the World Pooh Sticks Championships. The parish church of St Peter has a 14th-century belltower and a splendid display of aconites in winter.

7 Wittenham Clumps and Sinodun Hills These two small hills are correctly called the Sinodun Hills, but their wooded tops are more popularly known as Wittenham Clumps. They are part of the 250-acre (101-hectare) Little Wittenham Nature Reserve, which is designated a Special Area of Conservation, managed by the Earth Trust and consisting of woodland on the hills and surrounding grassland. Amongst the trees of Wittenham Clumps is a 'poetry tree' carved with the lines of a poem by a local man, Joseph Tubb, in 1844–5. *Wittenham Clumps* is also the title of a famous painting by the artist Paul Nash which hung in the Queen Mother's bedroom for many years.

The second of the Sinodun Hills, Castle Hill, is ringed by the massive banks of an early Iron Age hill fort. Both hills offer outstanding views of the surrounding countryside.

8 Dorchester Just a short diversion across the fields, Dorchester is a fascinating and historic place, having been built over a Romano-British town which grew by the Roman road from Silchester. Early Christianity thrived here, too. The great abbey church of St Peter and St Paul was built around 1140 on or near the site of a Saxon cathedral dedicated to St Birinus. The portions you see today survive because, in 1536, when the abbey was dissolved, a 'great riche man' of Dorchester, one Richard Beauforest, bought it and gave it to the people of the parish. Pilgrims along the Thames must surely pause here, especially for the glory of the 14th-century glass and the unique Tree of Jesse window, where tracery, sculpture and stained glass combine in a masterwork by an unknown hand. The nearby former

A classic Thames view – the church and bridge at Abingdon.

Abingdon

The ancient market town of Abingdon can base its success on commercial, academic and scientific developments and on the attractions of its riverside location. It is extremely old, with evidence of unbroken settlement through Iron Age, Roman and Saxon times. This has led to Abingdon's claim to be the oldest continuously occupied settlement in the country.

The traditions of the past are very much alive in the town today, through its annual Michaelmas Fair in October and Runaway Fair a week later, and its custom of celebrating significant and royal events by 'Bun Throwing' from the roof of the magnificent 17th-century County Hall. The famous Monday Market was established in the 14th century and a new monthly Farmers' Market, started in 2000, is now held on the third Friday in the month.

To explore Abingdon, go up the steps on either side of the bridge and walk up Bridge Street towards the town centre.

The centre of the town is dominated by the County Hall, built between 1678 and 1682 by Christopher Kempster. It is one of the finest examples of the architectural style of Christopher Wren. The cellars were used as a warehouse, the lower colonnade as a market, and the upper floor as a courtroom. Nowadays this building is home to the town museum, which is due to re-open in spring 2012 after a major refurbishment.

To the right of the Abbey Gateway are the Guildhall and its cluster of historic buildings. One of these housed a school re-established by John Roysse in 1563; others served as St John's Hospital for travellers and the poor. The Council Chamber of 1731 and the Roysse Room are of particular interest. On view in the Guildhall are many paintings and the Corporation Plate.

Next to Roysse Court is the Crown and Thistle, an old coaching inn dating from 1605. Its name commemorates the union of England and Scotland under James I. At the bottom of Bridge Street is the Old Gaol, built in 1811 by Napoleonic prisoners-of-war. It housed all prisoners for the County of Berkshire for 56 years, then in 1874 it was sold to a corn merchant who used it as his store for almost a hundred years. Facing the Old Gaol is Thames Street, at the far end of which is the narrow entrance to the few surviving buildings of the Old Abbey. The first room was once the Abbey Granary; beyond this lie the Checker, a fine 13th-century room, and the Long Gallery with its splendid oak-beamed roof. These buildings are open to the public at various times throughout the year.

From 1711 until 2000 the Morland Brewery, makers of the well-known Old Speckled Hen, was located in the town. Abingdon was also the proud home of the MG sports car and remains headquarters of the MG Car Club.

guesthouse, the last fragment of monastic building, houses a museum providing insights into the area's prehistory, right back to the crop-marks of 2500 BC. The High Street offers even more to see, including two fine coaching inns – evidence of Dorchester's importance as a staging post between London and Oxford.

9 **Shillingford** The Thames Path runs through this attractive village, which has several fine old buildings. You pass the aptly named Wisteria Cottage, its wisteria looking beautiful in flower and stretching some 50 yards along the house and barn. The peace and tranquillity of the riverside at the bottom of Wharf Road, with two benches next to a thatched boathouse, contrast greatly with the long,

forbidding walls of Shillingford Court, which are reluctant to reveal a fine old building. Note the historic tide levels marked on the corner of the building as you leave Wharf Road, the highest (in 1809) being above head height.

10 **Benson** A large settlement on the north bank of the river and close to the path, Benson is now a thriving commuter village and there is an RAF station nearby. Historically it was the location of some strategic battles during the English Civil War. Benson is famously known as a frost hollow, having recorded some of the lowest nightly temperatures in the country, and now has its own weather station. Look out for the curious anomaly in the numbers on the clock on the tower of St Helen's Church.

Route description

From the centre of **Abingdon** **1** cross the river bridge and take the steps down to the towpath. Your walk continues on a fine path through riverside gardens, with an excellent view of the spire of St Helen's Church and some of the surrounding almshouses – the earliest dating from 1446. Through a gate and across open meadows now, you cross a substantial footbridge **A** with a gate at one end, over the same Swift Ditch that left the Thames a long mile back (see page 74). From the footbridge, look left for an unchanged vision of medieval times: Old Culham Bridge, constructed at the same time as Abingdon Bridge, but now, unused and unrestored, peacefully sleeping more centuries away.

Now the riverside path skirts the vast, open field that virtually surrounds

Culham. At a sharp bend in your path, the old Thames channel leaves to meander via Sutton Courtenay, while you follow the lock cut. Approaching **Culham** **2**, the path narrows and becomes more enclosed and the hamlet gradually reveals itself across the fields to the left.

A footbridge over the cut carries a path that leads over the weirs of Sutton Pools to **Sutton Courtenay** **3**.

Another path on the left leads to Culham, but the Thames Path keeps resolutely on along the cut, past Culham Lock via two gates and up to the road.

From this point, Culham station is reached by walking left up the road, then right along the A415 for over a mile(1.6 km), passing the Waggon and Horses pub. There is another pub, the Railway Inn, near the station.

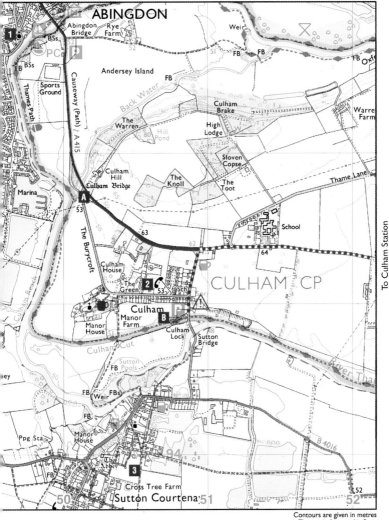

Contours are given in metres
The vertical interval is 5m

From Culham Lock access track **B**, your path forks right by the waterside to cross the road alongside the narrow lock-cut bridge and through the gate directly opposite. This is another bridge with one-way light control, so watch out for the traffic flow. Go ahead and down some steps and you will now be looking along an unusually straight, tree-hung reach, and very soon, back over your shoulder,

you can see the old loop of the Thames rejoining the cut, under the three-arched Sutton Bridge. Until the early 1800s, when both bridges and the lock cut were built, the barges had to follow this loop up to Sutton Courtenay village, then literally under a very obstructive Sutton Mill. Everyone must have seen the new cut as a big improvement except the miller, who thus lost his tolls.

Follow the riverside path, which undulates and can be muddy in parts after rain, until it becomes a rough, narrow way by the edge of fields. The towers of Didcot Power Station loom distantly over the river. Under more power lines and a very low railway bridge, barns, cottages and the unusual, fat spire of **Appleford Church 4** are just a field away over the Thames. Then, a pattern is repeated as a weir on the right takes an old loop up to Long Wittenham, and again you are following a lock cut.

Pass straight through Clifton Lock and the whole scene is transformed, opening out as though some artistic hand had composed the landscape. A red-brick Gothic bridge spans the river, a little church spire rising beyond it, while the rustic cottages of **Clifton Hampden 5** peep through a tasteful arrangement of trees. Walk on towards the bridge, where

your path goes left up to the road; but note that another path goes under the bridge and across the meadow beyond, should you want to visit the church. To the left now are the renowned cottages of Clifton Hampden with their steeply pitched, thatched roofs.

Across the bridge, just around a bend, is the Barley Mow, the best known of all Thames pubs, facing you as you approach.

Your route now crosses the bridge, where, once more, you need to watch the one-way traffic flow; then, on the other side, a path on the left goes through a gate and down steps to the river bank and open meadowland. This path is wonderful, as you stride the springy turf and a vast curve of the Thames swings round to **Little Wittenham 6**. You can measure your progress by noting the lie of the **Sinodun Hills 7** away over to the right, with the Thames flowing at their

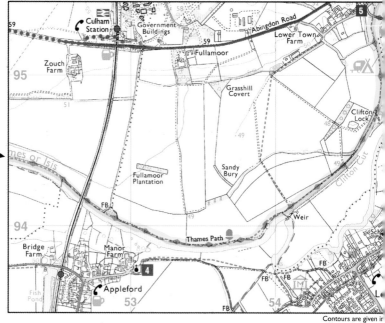

Contours are given in
The vertical interva

feet. Pass the elegant lawns and villas of Burcot, then, as you come nearer to the hills, the tower of the abbey church of Dorchester is seen rising above the trees to your left.

Under the tumbling branches of elderly willows, your path narrows as it comes up to Day's Lock, first crossing the weir **C** then the upper lock gates to the Dorchester bank. From the weir bridge you can see past the lock to **Wittenham Clumps 7**, with Little Wittenham Bridge tucked beneath, giving scale to the delectable scene.

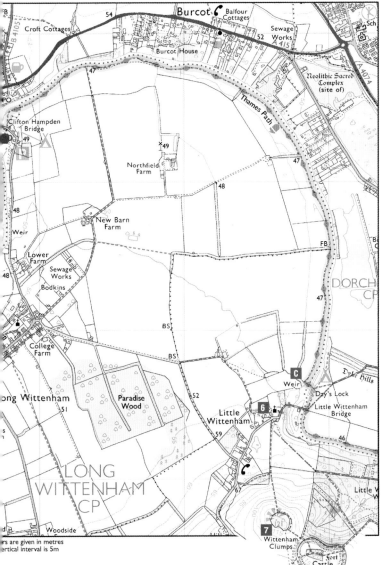

Contours are given in metres
The vertical interval is 5m

Walking along the grass by the lockside to the footbridge now, you have almost too many options as regards taking a detour.

Over the bridge and up the lane past Little Wittenham Church, a clear path up Church Meadow takes you to the summit beech clump of the nearer hill, Round Hill, which offers superb views.

Alternatively, a path from the footbridge leads, in a left diagonal, back across the meadow towards **Dorchester** **8**, *taking you first through a bridleway gate and then by an enclosed path running alongside the* *impressive ramparts of the Dyke Hills, the landward defences of a pre-Roman town.*

But these are diversions. The path continues through a gate under Little Wittenham Bridge and on through open meadowland by the river beneath Wittenham Wood, before crossing the meandering River Thame by a large footbridge with gates at either end, towards Shillingford. Before the village, the towpath comes to the site of Keen Edge Ferry. As you can no longer cross, a diversion away from the river is necessary. Beyond a brick pillbox, a fingerpost  points you, left, to the nearby main road through a wooden kissing-gate. Cross carefully to the footway on the far side and turn right. At the crossroads, with 🪧 The Kingfisher pub on one corner, turn right into Wharf Road, the charming village street of **Shillingford** 🟦. The point where the road ends at the Thames is a memorable spot, with, on one side, a thatched boathouse and, on the other, the stone and brick of Shillingford Court.

Just before the corner of Shillingford Court, your way goes left on a narrow path between walls 🟦. Joining another path at a T-junction, turn right, still keeping the Court wall to your right, pass the entry gates, carry straight on through a narrow metal kissing-gate and turn left up a drive to a busy road. Turn right in the road, but soon, just as you reach Shillingford Bridge, cross with care to drop down to a path leading to the river, then turn left on the towpath again.

Pause for a moment to look back at the elegant, three-arched bridge in its park-like setting. Carrying on, you will soon come into open fields with the distant line of the Chilterns escarpment way ahead. This path is narrow in parts.

Nash and Spencer

Paul Nash (1889–1946), the British landscape artist, had much in common with that other great 20th-century artist Sir Stanley Spencer. Both studied at the Slade School and went on to become war artists. Nash was a member of the Surrealist movement and loved to paint ancient sites such as Wittenham and Avebury.

enham Clumps,
nted by Paul Nash in 1935.

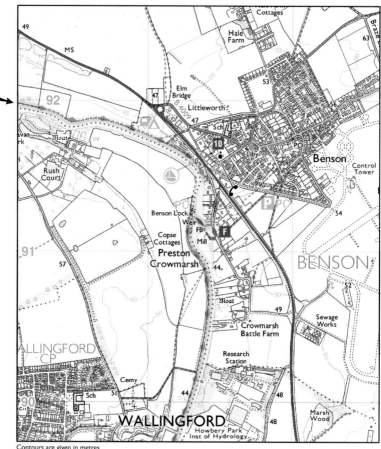

Contours are given in metres
The vertical interval is 5m

Around one more bend, you will see the moored craft of Benson cruiser station. Walk on over a small side-stream and through a metal gate into the marina and caravan area, all the time keeping near the riverside. Eventually you join a drive to skirt round a slipway. As you pass their sheds and cross grass, look out for the ☕ Waterfront Café on the left. Go through a kissing-gate into a small public garden, crossing it diagonally to another gate in the far corner. Turn right along the lane.

🚪 *Benson* 🔟 *and its church are to your left across the main road.*

Follow the lane towards Preston Crowmarsh. After some 300 yards (275 metres), you will see a 'footpath to the river' sign on your right – however, you should ignore it. Another 150 yards (140 metres) further on, with the sound of thundering water to guide you, turn right through a gate 🇫 leading directly to a footbridge over a millstream, and then to the crossing of the spectacular Benson

Weir. Over the weir, a perfectly clear path continues ahead over the lower lock gates. When you reach the far bank, go left for 30 yards (27 metres) and cross the ditch by a wooden footbridge, then turn left and follow the river along a broad fenced path.

In the past there was serious erosion along this bank, so the path you follow today was created on a new line, further back into the field. Ahead, a distinctive church spire seems to be imitating the line of poplars that frames it. This is St Peter's, which was given its open-work spire in the 18th century by Sir Robert Taylor. On sighting this, you know that you are approaching Wallingford.

Cross a wooden footbridge and soon, to your right, fragments of stonework on a grassy bank appear – all that remains of Wallingford Castle. It declared for the king in the Civil War, and was finally taken and demolished on the orders of Oliver Cromwell. Just short of the bridge, the towpath turns up right between walls, then left to the foot of the High Street, with 🍺 the Gate House pub on the corner.

The Thames Path heads right up the High Street and soon turns left into Thames Street.

🍺☕🏠 *To explore the historic heart of Wallingford (see page 94), continue ahead up the High Street.*

Public transport
Culham (1.6 miles/2.6 km) 🚆
Clifton Hampden (on route) 🚌
Dorchester (1.2 miles/1.9 km) 🚌
Wallingford (on route) 🚌
Taxis/minicabs: Clifton Hampden, Wallingford

Refreshments and toilets
Culham (0.3 mile/0.5 km) 🍺 Waggon and Horses
Sutton Courtenay (0.9 mile/1.4 km) 🍺 The Swan, George and Dragon
Clifton Hampden (on route) 🍺 Barley Mow, The Plough
Dorchester-on-Thames (1.2 miles/1.9 km) 🍺 Fleur de Lys, George Hotel, White Hart; ☕ Dorchester Abbey Tea Room (limited opening times)
Shillingford (on route) 🍺 The Kingfisher, Shillingford Bridge Hotel
Benson (on route) 🍺 Three Horseshoes, Crown Inn; ☕ Waterfront Café
Wallingford (on route) 🍺☕ wide selection

Food shops: Radley, Clifton Hampden, Wallingford
Public toilets: Culham Lock, Day's Lock, Wallingford

Accommodation
Culham (1.6 miles/2.6 km) Railway Inn
Sutton Courtenay (0.9 mile/1.4 km) Appletree Cottage, The Courtyard
Clifton Hampden (on route) Bridge House Caravan Site
Long Wittenham (1.6 miles/2.6 km) Witta's Ham Cottage, The Grange
Day's Lock (on route) campsite
Little Wittenham (0.1 mile/0.2 km) Keepers Cottage
Dorchester-on-Thames (1.2 miles/1.9 km) White Hart Hotel, George Hotel, Fleur de Lys
Shillingford (on route) Alouette, Kingfisher Inn, Marsh House, Shillingford Bridge Hotel, Bridge House
Benson (on route) Brookside, Crown Inn, Fyfield Manor, Benson Waterfront campsite
Wallingford (on route) George Hotel, Old School House, 52 Blackstone Road

7 Wallingford to Tilehurst

via Streatley, Goring and Whitchurch-on-Thames
14¾ miles (23.6 km)

This attractive and varied section starts in the old riverside town of Wallingford and passes through the Goring Gap – the dramatic valley carved by the River Thames through the line of chalk hills. It is the only section of the walk with anything like a serious hill, with one climb and one steep descent to negotiate through typical Chiltern countryside. The beech woodlands on this walk can look stunning on a crisp, sunny, autumn day and you may well be accompanied overhead by circling red kites. The regularity of rail connections allows greater flexibility to plan walks in this area. The final approaches to Tilehurst are quite a contrast, being much more urban in parts. At Streatley this section of the Thames Path crosses another long-distance route – The Ridgeway National Trail.

Transport options

Wallingford is well served by buses, with links to Reading, Oxford, Henley and Didcot Parkway. There are rail connections at Cholsey after 3¼ miles (5.1 km), Goring and Streatley after 7¼ miles (11.6 km), Pangbourne a further 4¼ miles (6.8 km) and finally at Tilehurst, meaning that shorter walks can be easily planned.

Things to look out for

1 Wallingford see page 94.

2 Cholsey The ancient settlement of Cholsey is located about a mile from the river south of Wallingford. It is claimed that this was the location of lands owned by the King of Wessex about AD 591. Near the church there is evidence of a Norman siege castle, but the church is better known as the final resting place of the author Agatha Christie, who lived nearby at Winterbrook. A tithe barn built at Cholsey in the 13th century was thought to be the largest aisled building in the world at the time; sadly it was demolished in 1815. Cholsey was once connected to Wallingford by a railway branch line known locally as 'The Bunk'. The line was closed to passengers in 1959 and to goods traffic in 1965, but continues to operate as a preserved line, running occasional diesel and steam services.

3 Moulsford An attractive group of cottages along the side of the A329 main road. From the trail you may glimpse the little church of St John the Baptist (not as old as it looks) down its drive by the river. When rebuilt in 1846, the wall facing you was the only fragment to be retained from what was possibly a 12th-century chapel. Moulsford is perhaps best known for its unusually named riverside inn, the Beetle and Wedge. The name is derived from the mallet (or beetle) and wedge used in wood-splitting and the tools are depicted on the inn's sign.

4 South Stoke Church As you rejoin the towpath south of Moulsford the tower of South Stoke church can be glimpsed across the river. The early 13th-century church of St Andrew has an attractive churchyard and serves a small parish which includes the ancient ferry crossing at Littlestoke. Although there are no direct links with the Thames Path here, South Stoke is on The Ridgeway National Trail and is a good location for walks.

5 Streatley With Goring-on-Thames opposite, this part of the river has always been an important crossing point. Two ancient trackways, The Ridgeway and the Icknield Way, crossed the Thames here, as did a Roman causeway and later a ferry. Neolithic and Bronze Age artefacts found at Streatley indicate early settlement at this spot. The village's one pub, The Bull, was mentioned by Jerome K. Jerome in *Three Men in a Boat* and there are stunning views of the Thames Valley from Streatley Hill.

6 Goring-on-Thames Sharing much ancient history with Streatley, Goring is the larger of the two villages that straddle the Thames. There are many historic buildings, including the church and mill, and Goring, which is surrounded by attractive countryside, has won many 'outstanding village' awards over the years.

7 Whitchurch-on-Thames This small but thriving village on the north bank of the river lies across from Pangbourne, to which it is linked by the Whitchurch Toll Bridge, one of two remaining toll bridges over the Thames. There has been a toll bridge here since 1792 and the current bridge was built in 1902. See Bridges, page 19.

8 Pangbourne A large village on the Thames, Pangbourne has many literary associations. Kenneth Grahame, author of *The Wind in the Willows*, retired here to Church Cottage, where he died in 1932, and The Swan public house is where an exhausted Jerome K. Jerome ended his *Three Men in a Boat* experience. A Falkland Islands Memorial Chapel in Pangbourne College is visited by the Queen on special anniversaries.

9 Hardwick House This Tudor-style mansion lies on the northern bank of the river to the east of Whitchurch. It is said that Charles I visited the house whilst under prison escort from Oxford. There is a polite dispute over whether Hardwick or Mapledurham (below) can claim to be the inspiration for E. H. Shepard's illustrations for Toad Hall in *The Wind in the Willows*.

10 Mapledurham Estate The whole community of Mapledurham, from the lock and mill to the church and the great Elizabethan manor house, evokes a wonderful 'time-passed-by' feeling. As mentioned above, there are gentle literary arguments between Hardwick House and Mapledurham House about which of these grand places appears in *The Wind in the Willows*. Mapledurham Water Mill, the last working water mill on the Thames, is open to the public and still produces quality stoneground flour. A turbine was installed in 2011 to produce green energy. The water mill famously appeared in the 1976 film *The Eagle Has Landed*. See Locks and Weirs, page 17.

The picturesque heart of ancient Wallingford.

Wallingford

Before you enter Wallingford you will pass on your right fragments of stonework on a grassy bank. These are the evocative remains of Wallingford Castle. Once one of the greatest medieval castles in England, it was built on the orders of William the Conqueror, who crossed the River Thames here in 1066. It dominated the Thames Valley for six centuries, surviving two civil wars in the process. It played a vital part in the English Civil War by declaring for the King, but was finally taken and demolished on the orders of Oliver Cromwell in 1652.

The town of Wallingford developed very early, as this has been a fording place on the river from prehistoric times. In fact it was the lowest point on the river where it was possible to cross at any season. The first bridge at Wallingford that we are sure about was completed in 1141, and Henry II granted the town a charter in 1155, making it the second town in the country to receive one. Wallingford was already important enough to house a royal mint and boast at least 10 churches. However, the town's prosperity declined in 1416 when

the new bridge was opened at Abingdon and revived only with the building of turnpikes in the 18th century.

From the river, a short walk up the High Street will bring you to the town museum in Flint House, a medieval hall-house, and opposite, on the open space called Kinecroft, you can still see the 9th-century earthworks that surrounded the Saxon town. Just past the fine 16th-century George Hotel with its courtyard, St Mary's Street leads left out of the High Street to the marketplace and the Town Hall, which dates from 1670. This

houses the Visitor Information Centre and is very much the heart of Wallingford.

For the TV detectives among you, the Corn Exchange Theatre doubles for the Causton Playhouse in the *Midsomer Murder* series. Even more famous, the crime writer Agatha Christie lived in the area and included Wallingford in many of her plots.

With its wide range of shops and services, combined with a fascinating history, Wallingford makes an excellent overnight stop on your Thames Path walk.

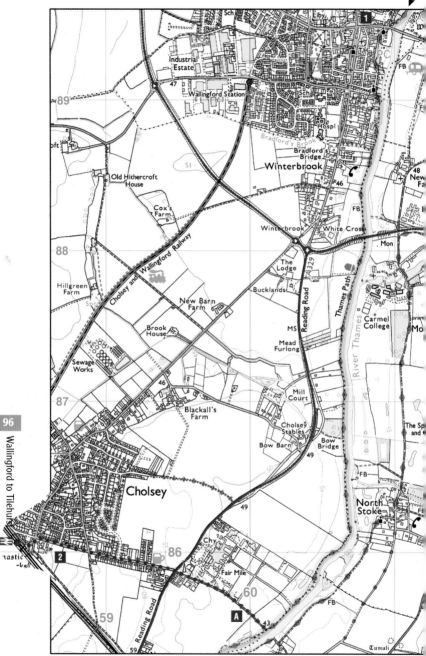

Sch
by
1
PC
FB

Industrial
Estate

47
Wallingford Station

89

Hospl

Bradford's Brook

oft

51

Old Hithercroft
House

Bradford's
Bridge

Winterbrook

Cox's
Farm

46

Winterbrook
White Cross

88

Mon

The
Lodge
A329

New
Fa

48

FB

Hillgreen
Farm

Cholsey and Wallingford Railway

Bucklands

Reading Road

Thames Path

New Barn
Farm

MS

Carmel
College

Mo

Brook
House

Mead
Furlong

River Thames

Sewage
Works

46

87

Blackall's
Farm

Mill
Court

Cholsey
Stables

The Sp
and

Bow Barn

Bow
Bridge

49

96

FB

Cholsey

49

North
Stoke

FE

2

86

Ch

Fair Mile

A

60

nastic

59

Reading Road

43

FB

Tumuli

59

Contours are given in metres
The vertical interval is 5m

Route description

The Thames Path turns right up the High Street in **Wallingford** 1, but very soon goes left into Thames Street, following it to the end where stands St Leonard's, oldest of the Wallingford churches. Just before the church, your path leaves on the left to skirt the churchyard, crossing a tiny brook to go through a terrace of cottages into a lane. Bear left here and, at once, you are back by the Thames again. Where the lane stops, your path narrows and continues, coming to the grass of a boatyard area. Keep by the waterside, go across the slipway and short footbridge, passing the new boathouse for the elite Oxford rowers, and return to the grass. Then go through a gap in the fence and continue on a narrow paved path, just a few yards back from the river, out into the open fields.

Under the bypass bridge, the towpath, narrow in parts, goes confidently on, across lawns, by meadows and through tree-belts – a tranquil stretch with the Chilterns now a continuous line beyond the river. Passing Oxford Brookes Rowing Club and a pair of large metal kissing-gates, take the path that continues ahead through a stock field. A grove of trees and traces of a landing stage across the Thames announce the location of Littlestoke Ferry, one of those points where our towpath once crossed to the far bank. An ancient track, the Papist Way A, comes down to the Thames on our bank.

▶ *For the village of **Cholsey** 2 and Cholsey station, turn right up this track, now called Ferry Lane. Keep straight ahead at the crossroads and for the station turn left at the next crossroads.*

The Thames Path approaches Goring Gap, with Goring Lock up ahead.

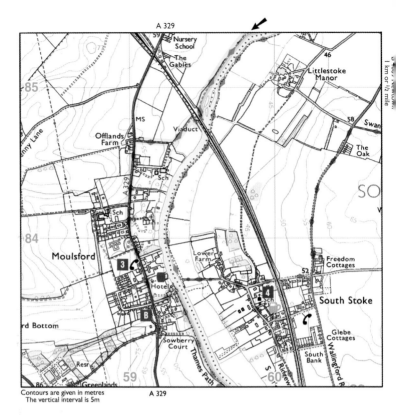

Contours are given in metres
The vertical interval is 5m

A 329

Between the old Littlestoke ferry point and the Beetle and Wedge, that errant towpath escapes to the other bank, so a walk away from the river via Moulsford will soon be necessary. From the ferry, the Thames Path keeps ahead by the river, through the greenery of Cholsey Marsh Nature Reserve, until the second of two wooden causeways takes you under the railway viaduct. There are two almost identical bridges here; the upstream one, Brunel's creation, is a superb example of skew brick construction. Beyond the bridge pass through a high metal gate in railings and a long narrow path leads through a large kissing-gate and on to a farm track up to join the A329 at Offlands Farm. Turn left here into **Moulsford** ■.

As the village ends, go left down Ferry Lane ■ to the river, bearing left via ▱ the Beetle and Wedge. At the river turn right, then continue by boat moorings and via a familiar brown gate on to the towpath. Soon you are in open meadows, the tower of South Stoke Church ■ across the river. This path is a delight, with great views of the Chilterns and springy turf underfoot. Beyond Cleeve Lock the walk is wooded for a while. Then after crossing a high, steep footbridge, the landscape opens up with hills framing the white house of Goring Lock. In the last field before the lock, the path goes diagonally right ■, leading to a wooden footbridge gated at one end and a path beyond, which soon becomes a narrow tree-lined avenue. At a path junction turn left on to a gravel track that runs past some white cottages, then twists right and left around Streatley Church before it reaches the road. You are now in 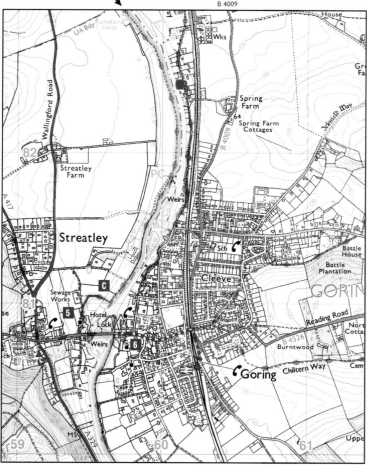**Streatley 5**; turn left and walk over the long bridge to reach **Goring-on-Thames 6** opposite.

For centuries this has been a river crossing. Today's long sequence of bridges and causeways, although mainly concrete, retains the character of an old trestle bridge on this significant line. Here you meet up briefly with The Ridgeway, which crosses the Thames before setting off along the Chilterns escarpment to Ivinghoe Beacon.

≈ *For Goring and Streatley station, keep ahead through Goring, over the railway line and turn right.*

Coming to the Goring bank, opposite the handy ≈ Pierreponts Café, cross the road with care then go down the steps on the right and return to the river, turning left on to the towpath again. A footbridge that crosses over the mill stream gives the briefest view of Goring

Contours are given in metres
The vertical interval is 5m

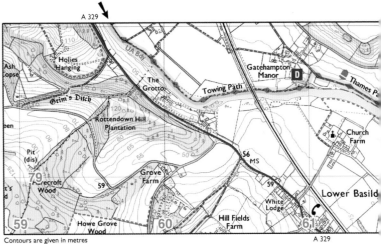

Contours are given in metres
The vertical interval is 5m

A 329

Church, then tree-clad hills descend to the Thames and you are into the Goring Gap, where, back in the Ice Age, the river cut itself a new channel through the chalk hills. This wonderful path passes tree trunks at all conceivable angles along the river bank. Cross another footbridge and to the right the dramatic slopes of the downs are high above you; in contrast, the Chilterns, with their characteristic hedgerows and beech-clad summits, come into view to your left only as you eventually emerge into open meadows.

Under the railway bridge – another one of Brunel's Great Western masterworks – and via an unusual kissing-gate, keep ahead along a fenced length of towpath towards Gatehampton Ferry Cottage, one more point where the old towpath crosses to the far bank beyond our reach. So, turn left over a footbridge **D** and, by a fence on the left, go up to a track and turn right. The track climbs slowly, clinging to a steep, roughly wooded bank, treating you, at one clear spot, to a surprise view of the Thames and the distant downs.

A chalk cliff requires the track to swing left and climb to the edge of the wood **E**. What follows is a pure Chiltern interlude, the hedged track dropping down into a typical dry bottom, then rising steeply up the other side to join the drive from Hartslock Farm. The long, broad drive ahead leads down to the road to **Whitchurch-on-Thames 7**. Turn right here and take care, especially on the parts without pavements, as you follow the road towards the Thames again.

The village street leads directly to the bridge, but the path turns right **F**, 75 yards (68 metres) beyond **D** The Greyhound pub, on to the drive to the church. Take the little path to the left of the lych-gate, cross the churchyard grass, and follow the path between walls until it comes out at Whitchurch Mill. Turn left here to walk past the pretty Church Cottages, turn right past the Toll House, then continue over Whitchurch Bridge. This is the second of two remaining toll bridges on the river, but there is no need to fumble for coins – pedestrians go free. See Bridges, page 19.

If you look back as you start across the bridge, you will see one of the picture-book Thames views – church, mill and cottages, ranged on the far side of the mill pool. Coming to the **Pangbourne** 8 side, walk on to the end of the white railings, then cross, go through a gap and turn left to cross the car park by the Adventure Dolphin Centre, continuing towards the National Trust-owned Pangbourne Meadow.

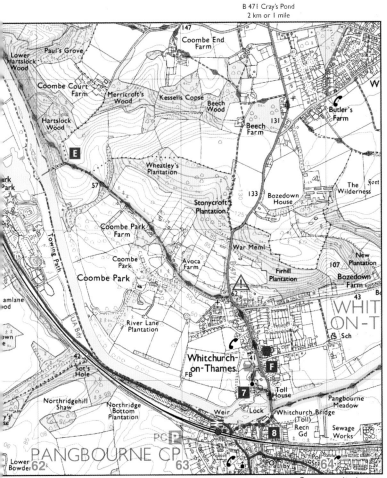

Contours are given in metres
The vertical interval is 5m

≷ For Pangbourne station, keep on up the road from the bridge and take the path to the right, which crosses the Pang, and gives a close-up view of the weir. On reaching a road, the station is to the right on the opposite side.

▱≷ The road over the bridge leads directly to the centre of Pangbourne.

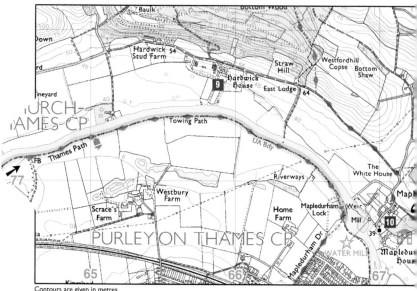

Contours are given in metres
The vertical interval is 5m

As you set forth from Pangbourne on open grassland, the Thames takes a vast curve with the Chiltern Hills as a backdrop over the river, terminating at Mapledurham Lock. Look out for a fleeting gap in the trees opposite, where the gabled **Hardwick House 9** can be seen over its lawns. **Mapledurham 10** itself is a delightful little community gathered around the Blount family mansion, but it can only be glimpsed through the trees on the far bank.

The tower of St Margaret's Church can be seen from some distance over the lock, then the corn mill, restored and working again, on its backwater. Beyond the lock, the great house can be sensed rather than fully seen through a veil of greenery. Mapledurham Lock is a delight, especially in summer, with lovingly tended flower beds; there is also a gallery of Thames scenes by a local artist, and a ☕ tea hut which, happily, is often open. A sign on the lock island tells you it is 78½ miles (126 km) to London, just in case you feel lost.

From here the path currently follows a temporary route. It is hoped that the final route, following more of the river bank, will be open before long. Please follow the signs. Go through a gate beyond the lock **G**, turn right along the field edge, then via another gate continue along a track, with the houses of Purley to your left. Follow this track, Mapledurham Drive, to its end, then continue up New Hill. Turn left and immediately right towards the railway bridge. Once over the bridge, turn left into Hazel Road **H** and follow it through Purley Park, up and down and around bends, eventually turning right into Skerrit Way. Where this road ends, steps on the right lead up to the A329. Turn left and follow the pavement to a large inn (closed for refurbishment in late 2011). A path to the left, just before it, leads over a railway bridge and down to the towpath to continue the walk.

≈ *For Tilehurst station carry on along the road for 400 yards (350 metres).*

Public transport
Cholsey (0.9 mile/1.5 km) ⇌
Goring & Streatley (0.7 mile/1.1 km) ⇌

Pangbourne (on route) ⇌
Tilehurst Station (on route) ⇌

Refreshments and toilets
Crowmarsh Gifford (0.3 mile/0.5 km)
🍺 The Bell, Queens Head
Cholsey (0.9 mile/1.4 km) 🍺 Morning Star, Red Lion
Moulsford (on route) 🍺 The Beetle and Wedge
Streatley (on route) 🍺 The Bull, The Swan
Goring-on-Thames (on route) 🍺 John Barleycorn, Miller of Mansfield, Catherine Wheel, Queens Arms; ☕ Pierreponts Café
Whitchurch-on-Thames (on route) 🍺 The Ferryboat, The Greyhound
Pangbourne (on route) 🍺☕ wide selection
Mapledurham Lock (on route) ☕ Tea Hut (seasonal opening times)

Food shops: Goring, Pangbourne,
Public toilets: Wallingford, Cleeve Lock, Goring-on-Thames, Pangbourne, Mapledurham Lock

Accommodation
Crowmarsh Gifford (0.3 mile/0.5 km) Little Gables, Riverside Park campsite, Bridge Villa campsite
North Stoke (1.9 miles/3 km) Springs Hotel
Cholsey (0.9 mile/1.4 km) 33 Ilges Lane
Moulsford (on route) Beetle and Wedge
South Stoke (2.6 miles/4.2 km) The Oak Barn
Streatley (on route) The Swan, Streatley YHA, 3 Icknield Cottages
Goring-on-Thames (on route) John Barleycorn, Lycroft, Melrose Cottage, Whitehouse at Wayland, Southview House
Pangbourne (on route) The George, Elephant Hotel, Weir View House,
Tilehurst Village (1.9 miles/3 km) 18 Partridge Drive, Firtrees

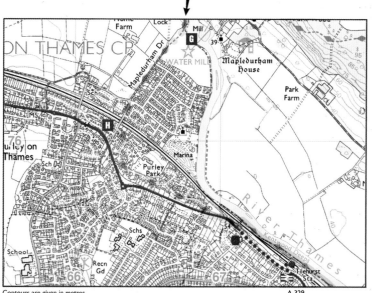

Contours are given in metres
The vertical interval is 5m

A 329

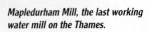
Mapledurham Mill, the last working water mill on the Thames.

8 Tilehurst to Henley-on-Thames

via Sonning and Shiplake
12¼ miles (19.7 km)

This section of the Thames Path is again very varied as it passes through the large urban centre of Reading on a surprisingly leafy route. It also takes in some quiet countryside and an area of flooded gravel pits. Highlights include the Sonning area and the exciting approach to Henley-on-Thames passing the River and Rowing Museum, a must visit for any Thames Path walker. The train links at Shiplake and Henley give an opportunity to plan shorter, circular walks. You may well spot red kites on this section, soaring majestically above the Thames Valley.

Transport options

From Tilehurst, a 3½-mile (5.5-km) stroll brings you to Reading with all its transport connections. Sonning 3¼ miles (5.2 km) further on has good bus links (except on Sundays) to Reading or on to Henley, Marlow or High Wycombe. Shiplake and Henley have railway stations on the Henley branch line to Twyford.

Things to look out for

1 Reading see page 108.

2 Caversham This large suburb of Reading spreads to the north of the Thames around Caversham Bridge. The 11th-century church of St Peter was damaged during the Civil War and Caversham Park House is home to part of the BBC World Service.

3 Kennet and Avon Canal An ambitious project to link Reading by boat with Bath and Bristol, the Kennet and Avon Canal was largely built during the 18th century but not completed until 1810 when the two river navigations were linked. Civil engineering highlights along the canal included the Crofton Pumping Station near Marlborough, the Caen Hill flight of locks at Devizes and the Dundas Aqueduct close to Bath. Competition from the railways sent the canal traffic into

decline and large sections became neglected and overgrown. However, a trust came to the rescue and has restored it magnificently, so today's towpath walk, all 87 miles (140 km) of it, is once more by a working canal.

For years, the spot where the Thames Path meets the Kennet – Kennet Mouth – lay under the threat of road schemes that would have swept away the historic Horseshoe Bridge and blighted the Thames hereabouts, but a famous victory in 1993 saved it.

Just a short distance from the Horseshoe Bridge is Blake's Lock, which, uniquely, is administered by the Environment Agency as if it were on the Thames. Next to the lock is a museum with exhibits about the River Thames and the Kennet and Avon Canal.

4 Sonning An attractive village that has grown around an ancient crossing point, Sonning is well worth the short diversion off the trail. It has some well-preserved old buildings and several fine hostelries. If you do walk through St Andrew's churchyard, note the massive buttressed walls of mellow, Tudor brick – all that remain of the palace of the Bishops of Salisbury, which once stood here. Next to the church stands the Deanery and Deanery Gardens, a Lutyens house with a Gertrude Jeykll garden, both designed in the classic Arts and Crafts style.

5 Shiplake Developed as two separate places, Shiplake itself consists of a cluster of cottages around the church, while Lower Shiplake, around the railway station, has grown into a large village. Shiplake is famous for hosting the annual Wargrave and Shiplake Regatta, which is second only in size to Henley. It also has some literary connections in that George Orwell lived here in his early days, while Jerome K. Jerome mentions Shiplake in *Three Men in a Boat*. In 1850 the poet Alfred Tennyson was married here in the 11th-century church of St Peter and St Paul.

6 Park Place On the approach to Henley, glance across the river to the grounds of a large estate rising up the hillside. This is Park Place, a Grade II-listed country mansion with a long and chequered history dating back to the early 18th century. Early owners included Frederick, Prince of Wales, eldest son of George II, while more recently it has been used as a boarding school and even featured in the remake of the St Trinian's film. The house achieved a certain fame recently when it was sold to a Russian billionaire for £140 million, making it Britain's most expensive house.

The centre arch of Sonning Bridge is a tight squeeze for big cruisers

Traditional and modern: houseboats moored along the Kennet and Avon Canal, with the buildings of Reading behind.

Thehurst to Henley-on-Thames

Reading

With its cutting-edge business parks Reading is a fast-growing town in the Thames Valley, but it also has a rich history. John Betjeman described it as a town that hides its past well. Over 1,000 years ago a huge battle between King Alfred's troops and the marauding Danes was fought in what is now the High Street. The church of St Mary conceals the ruins of an enormous abbey, larger than Westminster in its day; it was consecrated by Thomas à Becket, Archbishop of Canterbury, in 1164 and in the Middle Ages Reading became a destination for international pilgrimage as it could count the hand of the apostle St James amongst its relics. It was so important nationally that it became one of the few places to be a burial ground for royalty; Henry I was buried here in 1136, although it is not known exactly where. Tudor monarchs, including Henry VIII, were frequent visitors to Reading and Jane Austen was a pupil at the Abbey School. Other illustrious connections include the photography pioneer William Fox Talbot, who set up the first mass-production photo laboratory in the town, and Oscar Wilde, a resident at the time, was imprisoned in Reading gaol for 'social indiscretions'.

In more recent times the town's prosperity grew on the back of three great Victorian businesses – the three Bs: Huntley & Palmers biscuit factory, Simonds brewery and Sutton Seeds bulbs.

To discover more about Reading's long and fascinating history, it is worth stopping off to visit the town's museum, which also houses the only full-sized copy of the Bayeux Tapestry. Sights to look out for in the centre of Reading include the recently renovated Victorian formal gardens of Forbury, the town hall square and nearby St Leonard's Church. For younger walkers Reading is, of course, synonymous with the famous annual rock festival.

Route description

Beside the inn at Tilehurst, a path **A** leaves the A329 to cross railway lines by a footbridge with steps and drops steeply on further concrete steps to the Thames and its towpath below. At the bottom of the steps, just to your left, the old towpath ends, a reminder that it has just spent a mere quarter mile on the far bank, a manoeuvre that involved two ferries and hours of delay to the barge traffic, thanks to the cussedness of an 18th-century Purley landowner. Turn right now. 'Welcome to Reading' proclaims the sign, but Reading will not intrude for a while yet. Indeed, you seem to be alone here with the Thames and the Chiltern Hills across the water, with only the occasional reminder of the main railway line high on the bank above you.

Crossing the forecourt of a marine services depot, you leave the railway and swing left with the river through a small chicane and into open fields. Enjoy them while you can; **Reading 1** is around the corner, and soon the signs of civilization – benches, litter bins and tidy grass – tell you that you have joined the Thameside Promenade, with the tall buildings of the town over the field to the right. Now Caversham Bridge is in view and, across the river, lawns rise towards Caversham church – the tower you can just see amongst the trees – and the rest of **Caversham 2**. Keep along the surfaced path on the riverside past a big rowing clubhouse with a refreshment kiosk behind (open summer weekends only), and go through a tunnel under the bridge.

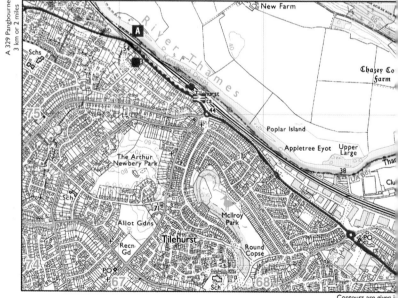

A 329 Pangbourne 3 km or 2 miles

Contours are given i
The vertical interva

Reading (see box, page 108) is an odd town, in that it stands on the Kennet rather than the Thames, and has never quite worked out a relationship with the river. Between the two bridges of Reading, industry has now given way to a pleasant mix of old and new housing, so your walk is enjoyable enough, taking you on to pass under Reading Bridge through a short tunnel.

🚪 ☕ ⇄ *To visit Reading town centre and for Reading station, go under the bridge, turn right up the steps to the road and go ahead via pedestrian crossings to walk under the railway bridge. On the other side, paths lead up to a footway that crosses the main road alongside the railway lines and continues into the station foyer. The town centre is very close to the station.*

Comedian David Walliams at Caversham Lock in September 2011, urged on by a cheering crowd, during his 140-mile swim of the Thames to raise money for Comic Relief.

Tilehurst to Henley-on-Thames

rs are given in metres
ertical interval is 5m

Beyond Reading Bridge, take the tarmac drive which leads past Caversham Lock and out into the expanse of King's Meadow. The sense of escape here is a little premature, as Reading still has a supermarket and a mighty gasholder to contribute to the Thames environment. But beneath the gasholder you come to that significant spot where the **Kennet** ❸ enters the Thames, and your towpath crosses it via the gaunt old Horseshoe Bridge, until recently a slatted horse bridge but now re-decked and more comfortable for our feet.

Beyond the Kennet, walk on by the riverside, trying to ignore the office developments that come painfully near. Beyond a boathouse the surfaced path ends and the grass underfoot comes as a welcome relief. Then, over a footbridge, and as the open meadow ends, you come to a wetlands nature reserve, with paths wandering off around its ponds, returning to the towpath a little further on. Once into the trees, you have the grounds of Reading Blue Coat School above you, and surprising glimpses of skimming sails and lagoons across the river where flooded gravel workings have been put to new use. Then carry on past Sonning Lock, a pretty, tree-circled location with urns and flowerbeds to admire, and continue by the access road to Sonning Bridge.

▶ *Before the bridge, you might be tempted to follow the path to the right, which passes the church, taking you into the village of **Sonning** ❹ by the attractive Bull Inn.*

It is the old, red-brick bridge in its lovely setting which draws the village together. A boundary plate on the centre arch confirms that it spans a county boundary, one half being in Oxon, the other in Berks. This may

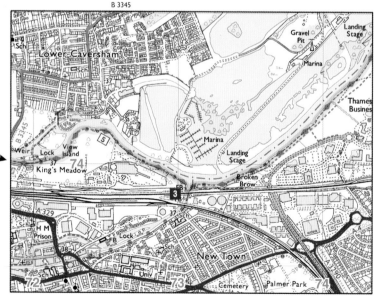

Contours are given in metres
The vertical interval is 5m

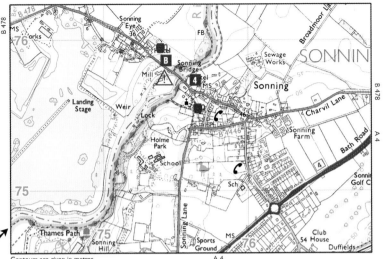

Contours are given in metres
The vertical interval is 5m

A 4

explain its quirky construction – eleven arches, all of different sizes, spanning the main Thames channel.

The Thames Path turns left across the narrow, humpback Sonning Bridge; again watch out for the light-controlled traffic-flow here. On the north side, take the big concrete bridge on your right over a weir stream **B** and through a gate to the towpath. Some of this water once powered Sonning Mill, an 18th-century flour mill now converted to a theatre and restaurant, and worth a stroll up the road to view. Below Sonning, the towpath is narrow in parts and slippery when wet; it is just a simple country way for a while, with loops and verdant backwaters of the Thames creating a constantly changing scene – a fine stretch.

The 16th-century Bull Inn at Sonning: 'a veritable picture of an old country inn' – Jerome K. Jerome.

The route to Henley-on-Thames

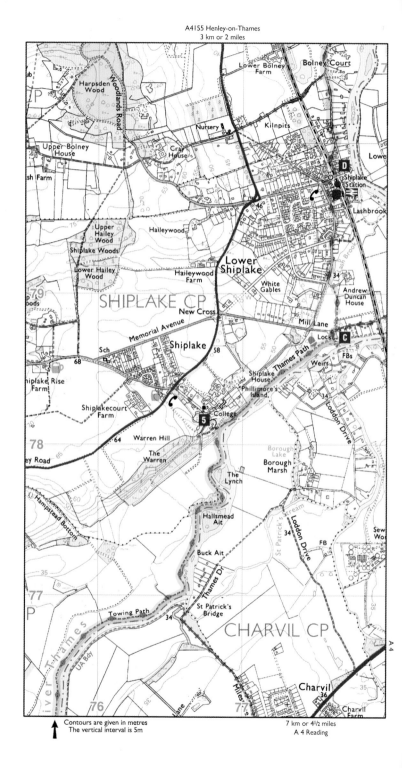

Contours are given in metres
The vertical interval is 5m

7 km or 4½ miles
A 4 Reading

A distant line of high ground comes gradually down to the river, and when they meet you will know you are at **Shiplake**  **5**. A once gated footbridge takes you in front of a handsome boathouse to a little lawn where you will often encounter the boys of Shiplake College and their boats.

📖 *Shiplake itself, just a cluster of cottages around the church, is high above you and can be reached by a path just beyond the footbridge, which goes left by the boathouses then steeply up the chalky bluff to the top. The Plowden Arms is located a short distance along the A4155 towards Reading.*

Shiplake College boathouse

The towpath continues over the grass and by the river; above, in the trees, are the college buildings (built as Shiplake Court in 1905). Approach Shiplake Lock through a large kissing-gate along a meadow sloping to the water's edge. A further large kissing-gate takes you into a metalled track leading up from the lock, where you turn left (the footbridge on the right leads only to the lockside). Coming into a lane, turn right for 25 yards (20 metres) then left along a field path **C**. This is currently a temporary route; it is hoped that the final route, following more of the river bank, will be available before too long. Please follow the signs. Continue on this path with a fence to your left. As the field ends, the path wriggles left through a kissing-gate, then crosses diagonally over the corner of another field to another kissing-gate and steps up into a lane. Turn left over a bridge, then right in the road to walk via Lashbrook to Lower Shiplake, the larger of the two settlements that make up Shiplake. While passing the cottages of Lashbrook, you may notice, down a drive

to the right, a white, boarded, barn-like building with a simple cross over the door – the Lashbrook Chapel. The road comes to a crossroads with the 📖 Baskerville Arms on one corner *and* ⇌ *Shiplake station just to your right.*

At Shiplake, your truant towpath crosses to the other bank at Lashbrook Ferry, returning again via Bolney Ferry after less than a mile (1.6 km), and as we cannot follow it, a diversion away from the river is necessary. Turn right at the crossroads and walk over the level crossing at Shiplake station, turning left on a grassy path **D** between the railway and house gardens. After 150 yards (140 metres), where a path comes over the line from the left to join yours, bear right through an old metal kissing-gate and follow a narrow path between gardens to a road, where you turn left. Along this attractive, tree-lined way, you can admire some impressive houses; those on the right are actually on the Thames.

The road bears right and you come to some gates, at which point a footpath 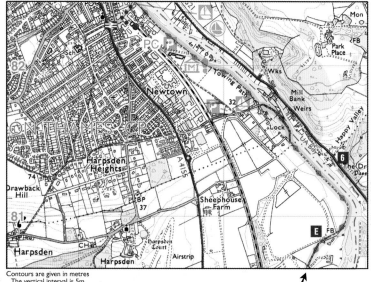 E continues to the left, fenced off from the drive and from open fields. Beyond the drive, a miniature railway runs by the garden edge – it even has a miniature station. The path continues, still fenced, over a crossing track and a footbridge into riverside meadows, where you bear left. This is the site of Bolney Ferry, so the towpath returns to our bank and you can follow it to Marsh Lock. Iron studs were placed along this meadow in 1903 to define the 14-foot (4-metre) width of the towing path. Only one seems to have survived, tottering on the river's edge as an indication of the extent of bank erosion here. Across the river, the grounds of **Park Place 6** rise and display odd features, including a cyclopian bridge of huge rocks, which you can see on the estate road up from the Thames.

Marsh Lock is unusually situated in midstream and you reach it via a long, wooden causeway, which is obviously a favourite seagull perch. Then, go past the Georgian lock house (very handsome with hanging flower baskets), and back to the bank again by a second causeway leading to pretty cottages at the foot of Mill Lane. Turning right on the riverside, past the Old House, you enter Mill Meadows, a popular promenade with all the usual accessories of memorial seats, bye-laws and doggie bins galore. ☕ Henley Piazza Café (opening times vary) stands across the grass to your left and there are toilets in the sports rotunda. Here you will find the stunning building that houses the River and Rowing Museum, where you can find out more about the Thames.

Henley seems constantly abustle with every activity connected with boats, and they are moored in rows as you pass the landings of Hobbs & Sons. A

Contours are given in metres
The vertical interval is 5m

walkway is clearly defined along the waterfront until  the Angel on the Bridge blocks the way, by which time you are at Henley Bridge.

To explore the bright little town of Henley-on-Thames, turn up Hart Street to the Market Place with its Victorian town hall.

Public transport

Reading (on route)
Sonning (on route) (not Sundays)
Shiplake (on route)
Henley-on-Thames (on route)

Refreshments and toilets

Reading (on route) wide selection
Sonning (on route) Bull Inn, Great House
Shiplake (0.5 mile/0.8 km) Plowden Arms
Lower Shiplake (on route) Baskerville Arms
Henley-on-Thames (on route) wide selection

Food shops: Reading, Lower Shiplake, Henley-on-Thames
Public toilets: Reading, Sonning Lock, Shiplake Lock, Henley-on-Thames

Accommodation

Reading (on route) wide selection – contact Visitor Information Centre
Sonning (on route) Bull Inn, Great House
Charvil near Reading (1.3 miles/2 km) Wee Waif Lodge
Lower Shiplake (on route) Crowsley House, Baskerville Arms
Henley-on-Thames (on route) wide selection – contact Visitor Information Centre

The towpath gets busier on the approaches to Henley – a classic Thames view.

9 Henley-on-Thames to Marlow

via Hurley

8½ miles (13.7 km)

This short section starts and finishes in attractive riverside towns – make sure you allow extra time to explore them. There is much to see along the way, from the drama of the Henley Regatta course to small hamlets full of historic interest. There is one short climb away from the river at Aston and the Chiltern Hills provide a beautiful natural backdrop throughout the walk. You may well be accompanied on your journey by a red kite or two. Parts of the route can be busy in summer and of course avoid the first week of July if you want to miss the Henley Regatta crowds.

Transport options

Henley is served by a branch railway line from Twyford. After 2½ miles (4 km) you come to Hambleden Lock, where from Mill End there are regular bus services back to Henley and Reading and on towards Marlow and High Wycombe. A further 3¾ miles (6 km) brings you to Hurley, from where occasional buses run to Henley or Maidenhead, Mondays to Saturdays. Marlow is served by a branch line from Maidenhead.

Things to look out for

1 Henley-on-Thames See page 120.

2 Remenham This small, attractive village on the banks of the Thames boasts two famous rowing clubs. The Leander Club, founded in 1818, is one of the oldest rowing clubs in the world, while the Remenham is a private members' club. St Nicholas Church in Remenham dates from the 13th century but was almost entirely rebuilt in 1870. There are few remains today of the Manor House, but the whole village with its attractive trees makes a most pleasing composition.

3 Temple Island The starting point for the Henley Regatta races. The small temple building dates from 1771 and is actually a fishing lodge with a cupola on top sheltering a nude lady. It was

designed by James Wyatt as a landscape feature to enhance the view from nearby Fawley Court, but the naked lady's view up to distant Henley must itself be breathtaking. (See Islands, page 22.)

4 Greenlands The present house, a gleaming white Italianate mansion, was built in 1853 on the site of a much earlier house for W. H. Smith, the bookseller, who became Viscount Hambleden. Jerome K. Jerome was a bit dismissive of the place in *Three Men in a Boat*. Today it is part of the Henley Business School and a very popular wedding venue.

5 Hambleden Mill The big weatherboarded mill dominates the landscape around Hambleden Lock and weir, and is very accustomed to the clicking of appreciative tourist cameras. The mill was driven by a water turbine and only ceased working in 1955. It is now divided into flats.

6 Hambleden To the north of Mill End lies the attractive village of Hambleden with its brick and flint cottages, 14th-century church and Jacobean Manor House.

7 Medmenham and the Hellfire Club There is an air of mystery surrounding Medmenham Abbey, with its hint of romantic ruin and its scandalous associations with Sir Francis Dashwood and the Hellfire Club. Dashwood, an 18th-century MP who was alleged to be a Jacobean spy and anti-Catholic, was passionate about what we might today call 'theme clubs'. As a result, he leased what was left of a 12th-century Cistercian abbey and converted it into the Gothic creation we see today on the north bank of the Thames. The Hellfire Club was thus established in 1749 as a place of drunkenness and debauchery, with mock religious ceremonies and extravagant costumes. Members – known as the Knights of St Francis – tended to be politicians, and Frederick, Prince of Wales (son of George II), the Earl of Sandwich and the artist William Hogarth were reputed to be members. Benjamin Franklin was a friend of Sir Francis Dashwood and may well have visited the Abbey. Eventually the antics of the club became too notorious and its activities were transferred to the remarkable series of underground caves at West Wycombe. These were dug by villagers near Sir Francis Dashwood's estate, giving employment to workers during a series

of poor harvests, and the Hellfire Club, with increasing notoriety, continued to operate there for some years. The whole episode remains steeped in mystery and legend to this day. The caves of West Wycombe are open to the public and well worth a visit.

8 Hurley Located just a short distance from the Thames Path, Hurley is a most attractive village and worth a detour. A short walk along an adjoining footpath brings you to a little parcel of green with, on the right, one of Hurley's two tithe barns, which has been converted into a house with a circular, 14th-century dovecote alongside. The second barn is just along the village street and a little further up is the marvellous Olde Bell, which claims to date from 1135. A priory was established here in the 11th century, and traces remain on the other side of the green. The parish church of St Mary the Virgin, with its long, narrow nave, was the priory chapel, and the quadrangle beside it contains parts of the refectory block.

9 Bisham Abbey Most of what can be seen across the river is a Tudor manor house built here by Sir Philip Hoby using fragments of the original abbey, which was built for the Knights Templar in 1260. It has associations with Henry VIII, who left the house to Anne of Cleves as part of her divorce settlement, and Elizabeth I was a regular visitor. Nothing remains today of the Abbey Church, known as Bisham Priory, which was the resting place for the Earls of Salisbury. Today Bisham Abbey has been given a new lease of life as Sport England's National Sports Centre and is a popular wedding venue.

Henley-on-Thames

This fine riverside town was founded in the 12th century and has a long and varied history. It boasts a Thursday market that has been going strong since 1269.

Henley, of course, is world-famous for rowing and the Henley Regatta has been a highlight of the social calendar for many years. The Regatta course is 1 mile 450 yards (2 km 21 metres) of remarkably straight Thames, descended upon by the rowing world every year in the first week of July. For some weeks either side of Royal Regatta week the stands and hospitality marquees transform this reach, and the riverside path may be diverted to a line back from the river. If you aim to enjoy the beauty of Henley Reach without diversions, best strike these weeks out of your diary. It is worth noting that the first Oxford versus Cambridge race was rowed along this reach in 1829, before moving to the familiar course from Putney to Mortlake, which you will encounter later on your journey along the Thames. Sensing the town was on to a good thing, a public meeting in Henley Town Hall established the Regatta 10 years later.

In 1998 the Queen opened the River and Rowing Museum on the Thames at Henley in a stunning building designed by architect David Chipperfield. It is a celebration of the river from source to mouth, the rowing traditions of Henley and the history of the town itself.

The town also has a brewing tradition that goes back more than 200 years. The River Thames was a major trade route, taking grain and timber from Henley to London and bringing in raw materials to the local craftsmen. Barley from the area was malted in one of the many malt houses. In 1823 Henley-on-Thames was home to at least 12 maltsters, and so far historians have discovered 42 malt houses within the town's boundary. The maltsters had little trouble selling on their end product, as nearly as many brewers set up shop to make use of the malted barley they produced. In 1854 at least five breweries were taking the local raw materials and creating ales and lagers for local consumption. They were: Greys Brewery on Friday Street, Cannon Brewery behind The Argyll pub, Crown Brewery in Market Place, Union Brewery and Ives Brewery.

As with most industries, Henley eventually saw its breweries merge with each other or be sold on, leaving only one brewer for most of the 20th century. Brakspears Brewery was founded in 1779 and continued to brew in Henley until the site was sold in 2002. Brewing of the Brakspear brands continues today in Witney.

A new brewery, Lovibonds, was started in 2005, proudly continuing Henley's brewing heritage.

Take time to explore this fascinating and lively town before continuing on your Thames Path walk.

Along the riverside at Henley, hireboats line up to await custom, and the towers of the Brakspear Brewery peep over the roofline of mellow Georgian houses.

Route description

Henley **1** looks its sparkling best from the other bank, and the Thames Path crosses the elegant 1780s bridge, allowing you to enjoy the view of the bridge, river front and the tall, 16th-century tower of St Mary's – a much-photographed Thames view. Over the bridge, cross at the pedestrian island and follow the path that turns sharply back to the riverside **A**. You are now looking down the Henley Regatta course.

The towpath has a metalled surface for most of the way, provided for the coaches of rowing crews to cycle along. You cross one high footbridge and pass Remenham and Upper Thames rowing clubs before the meadows open up, and a pretty string of brick cottages of **Remenham 2** is followed by the low, flint tower of the church appearing over the trees. You can visit by means of a gate into the lane opposite the church. Ahead, the long

Regatta reach is terminated by a tiny temple on **Temple Island 3**.

Beyond Temple Island and over a cattle grid, the river bends sharply towards Hambleden Lock, soon passing, across the river, the grounds of the Italianate mansion of **Greenlands 4**. Now on a grass surface, a gate takes you along the lock side, with views across the series of weirs to **Hambleden Mill 5**.

🍴 🚌 *For a closer view (or to reach the Mill End bus stop), a right of way crosses the lower lock gates and the spectacular white water of Hambleden Weir. From here the village of **Hambleden 6** can be reached via a footpath from the minor road north of Mill End. The village pub, the Stag and Huntsman, is closed for refurbishment until May 2012.*

Continue ahead past the lock and through a kissing-gate, then follow the access road for a short way, before

Temple Island is the starting point for the Henley Regatta races, facing up the long Regatta reach with the Chiltern Hills rising in the distance

leaving it to go through a gate on the left. Continue by the riverside to Aston Ferry on a wonderful stretch through open meadowland. Here, by the ferry landing, the towpath departs for the other bank for a while, so turn right up Ferry Lane **B** past the attractive cottages

of Aston hamlet to 🛑 The Flowerpot. This inn has an Edwardian feel to it, the bar full of fish in cases, and often with anglers too, and the legend outside announces: 'Good accommodation for fishing and boating parties'. Pass the inn, carry on up Aston Lane for 75 yards (68

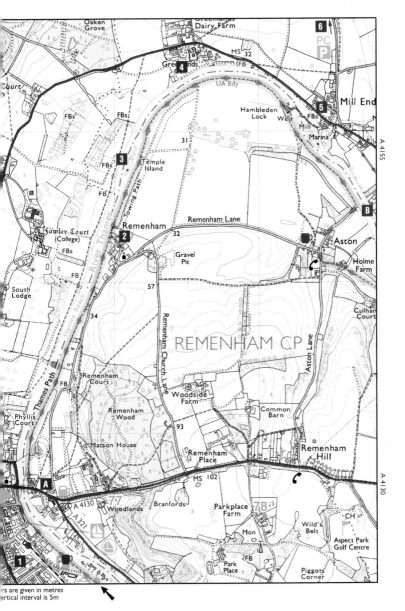

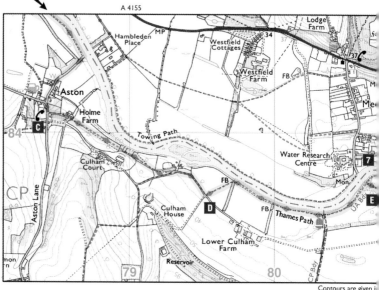

Contours are given i
The vertical interva

metres), then turn left along a drive that climbs past Holme Farm until, where it turns right, your path keeps ahead through a gate and into an open field. From the clear path there are magnificent views to the left over the Thames Valley, and ahead to the red-brick, 18th-century Culham Court on its rise. The path goes below it via kissing-gates, then ahead over an open meadow which is being developed as a deer park. Keep ahead following signs and lead into a track, where you turn left for 100 yards (90 metres) towards cottages, then right along a gravel track. When this track comes to a farm road at a corner, go half-left through a wooden kissing-gate and over a field .

Once more you are back by the Thames, and you can follow the bank again through open meadowland via several more gates and footbridges for a long half-mile until, just to your left, you can see traces of a ferry landing stage. You have reached **Medmenham 7** and just

across the river, best viewed from a few paces on, is Medmenham Abbey.

From the ferry landing, the Thames Path takes an unexpected short-cut along the track that heads off diagonally through a kissing-gate across the fields and through another kissing-gate to rejoin the towpath. Ahead, near two islands, are the big barns of Frogmill, residential now, but characterful with their stone-and-flint patterning. The waymarked path keeps by the water's edge until it is forced to join a gravel drive past houses and bungalows before reaching open meadows again. The big, white, castellated mansion ahead, gazing down in proprietorial fashion from its high, chalk cliff, is Danesfield, built around 1900 and now a hotel.

Approaching Hurley, the riverside in summer tends to be overpopulated by picnic parties, but as the picnic meadow ends and its access road swings away, a weir signals the close presence of Hurley Lock. Your path continues by the river's

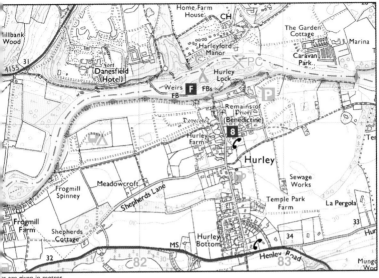

's are given in metres
rtical interval is 5m

edge. Passing through an old metal gate, you come to a rustic bridge over the lock cut. Turn left over the bridge and on to the lock island .

📖 🚌 Another path on the right just before the bridge leads, rather delightfully, over a stream, past cottages into the village of Hurley ⑧ just a few minutes away.

Having crossed the rustic bridge, you can roam the lock island at will; this is an open picnic area with toilets behind the lock cottage and 🍵 a teashop with limited opening times. Beyond the lock, a second rustic bridge returns you to the river bank. As you walk on, look back to see Harleyford Manor – a handsome little house built in 1755 – just glimpsed between islands, where it now serves as a clubhouse for the marina.

...magnificent church of St Mary ...Virgin in Hurley village is ...ted close to the path.

Ahead now, through two gates and a meadow, is Temple footbridge, which spans the Thames 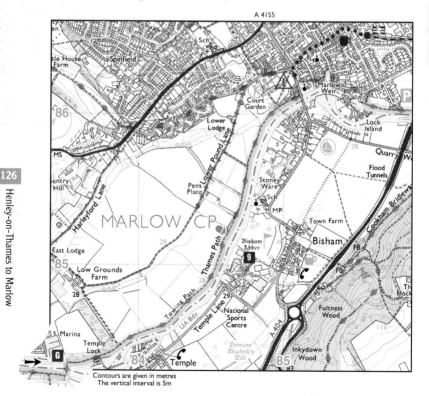 on the line of the ferry that closed in 1953. This graceful 150-foot (46-metre) wooden arch was opened in 1989, very effectively solving one of the Thames Path's crossing problems. Cross it gratefully and walk on along the towpath, surfaced now, through gates to pass Temple Lock and the modern housing that replaces the mills on Temple Island. Keep on the access road and then the towpath again through open meadowland with a clear path ahead to Marlow.

Soon, **Bisham Abbey** 🔟, followed by Bisham Church, make a mellow composition across the river. Cross two short but surprisingly steep footbridges and a last bend brings Marlow into view,

the pinnacled church spire and delicate line of the suspension bridge making another classic river view.

The approach to Marlow is unexpectedly rural along a fenced towpath past open fields. Finally a footbridge brings you into Higginson Park and the town promenade. Walk right up to the bridge and admire its detail, then turn left up the slope to the main street. The Thames Path continues across the road on the north side of All Saints Church.

To explore Marlow (see box, page 131) turn left up the High Street towards the town centre. For Marlow station, walk up the High Street and turn right down Station Road. At the Marlow Donkey pub go half-right down Station Approach to the well-hidden platform.

Contours are given in metres
The vertical interval is 5m

...ugh the trees on the opposite ...k, Medmenham Abbey has a ... of romanticism.

Public transport

Mill End near Hambleden (0.2 mile/0.3 km) 🚌
Hurley-on-Thames (on route) 🚌 (not Sundays)
Marlow (on route) 🚆 🚌

Refreshments and toilets

Aston (on route) 🍺 Flowerpot Inn
Hurley-on-Thames (on route) 🍺 Ye Old Bell, Rising Sun; ☕ Hurley Lock Tea Shop (limited opening)
Marlow (on route) 🍺☕ wide selection
Food shops: Henley-on-Thames, Hurley (limited opening), Marlow

Public toilets: Henley-on-Thames, Mill End, Hurley Lock, Temple Lock, Marlow

Accommodation

Aston (on route) Flowerpot Inn
Frog Mill (0.5 mile/0.8 km) Black Boys Inn
Hurley (on route) Hurley B&B, Meadow View, Hurley Riverside Park campsite, Hurley Lock campsite
Bisham (1.2 miles/1.9 km) The Old Vicarage
Marlow (on route) wide selection – contact Visitor Information Centre

10 Marlow to Windsor

via Cookham and Maidenhead
14¼ miles (23 km)

This long and varied section passes through some attractive countryside with views of the wonderful woodland of the Cliveden Estate, especially colourful in autumn, between Cookham and Maidenhead. The village of Cookham, with its Stanley Spencer associations, is well worth a visit. Beyond the bustle of Boulters Lock and the busy town of Maidenhead, the peaceful towpath returns. You pass close to one of the 2012 Olympic venues – the rowing lake at Dorney. Unfortunately, due to the Olympic Games there is a diversion away from the towpath here, which may remain in place until late 2012. The walk finishes with a dramatic view of Windsor Castle from across the meadows near Eton.

Transport options

From Marlow you pass near Bourne End station after 3¼ miles (5.1 km), then Cookham after another 1¼ miles (2 km); both are served by the Marlow branch from Maidenhead. Maidenhead, with rail connections to London, is a further 3¼ miles (5.1 km). Windsor, at the end of this section, has two stations, offering either a shuttle service to Slough or direct services to London Waterloo.

Things to look out for

1 Marlow See box, page 131.

2 Bourne End A large, thriving commuter village on the north side of the river which boasts several pubs and restaurants but is probably best known for its literary associations. In the 1920s it was home to two famous writers – children's author Enid Blyton and Edgar Wallace, the crime writer.

3 Cock Marsh This expanse of marshland and grass between Winter Hill and the Thames is owned by the National Trust and has been common land since 1272. It is one of the best lowland wetland sites in the country and is important for flora and a wide range of wading birds. It is still grazed in the traditional manner.

4 Cookham See box, page 132.

5 Cliveden There has been a house here since the mid-17th century. The original was destroyed by fire in 1849 and the Italianate mansion that replaced it, set high above the Thames in beech woodland, was designed by Sir Charles Barry in the 1850s. Cliveden has been visited by almost every British monarch since George I. It was bought by William Waldorf Astor in 1893 and gained a colourful reputation for political intrigue and scandal, especially in the 1920s and 1930s, when Nancy Astor hosted a group known as the 'Cliveden Set' – politically influential members of the upper class who met to discuss opinions and ideologies in inter-war Britain. The views and beliefs of the Cliveden Set are a matter of some dispute, but it has been suggested that they had links with the German aristocracy and in fact supported Nazi Germany. The house again gained a reputation for notoriety in the 1960s, when the Profumo affair focused world attention on one of those innocent riverside cottages on the estate. The MP John Profumo had an affair with Christine Keeler, supposedly simultaneously the mistress of an alleged Russian spy. He subsequently lied about it in the House of Commons, seriously weakening Harold Macmillan's government.

Today Cliveden House is owned by the National Trust and leased to a hotel chain, but the grounds and occasionally parts of the house are open to the public. The estate stretches down the steep hillside to the river bank and the beech woodlands make a magnificent sight in the changing colours of autumn.

6 Boulter's Lock This lock, near Maidenhead, is probably the most famous on the whole of the River Thames. It was formerly called Ray Mill Lock, so named as there used to be a mill here owned by the Ray family. 'Boulter', or 'bolter', is an old English word for a miller, and indeed the mill race still rushes underneath the lock.

Back in the Edwardian days of punts and parasols, this was the most fashionable spot on the Thames, especially on Ascot Sunday, when as many as a thousand small craft would parade, in a series of regattas, through the lock beneath an admiring audience.

7 Maidenhead A very busy and affluent commuter town in the Thames Valley, Maidenhead is part of the so-called 'Silicon Corridor'. It has grown due to its strategic location on the river, the first bridge having been built here in 1280. Once an important stop on the London to Bristol coaching route, it developed further with the arrival of the Great Western railway in the early 19th century. The town was gently 'ridiculed' by Jerome K. Jerome in *Three Men in a Boat.*

The town centre has a wide range of shops and restaurants, and the Maidenhead Heritage Centre highlights aspects of the history of the town in a series of special exhibitions.

8 Bray Just across the river on the outskirts of Maidenhead lies the small village of Bray. Despite its closeness to Maidenhead, it retains a wonderful old English village atmosphere and has a unique position in the gastronomic geography of Britain, boasting not one but two top-quality Michelin-starred restaurants. There is the Fat Duck, of Heston Blumenthal fame, which has three stars; while the nearby Waterside

Lady Astor with George Bernard Shaw at Cliveden in 1941.

Under starter's orders in the Men's Eights at the 2008 World Rowing Championships on Dorney Lakes.

Inn, run by the Roux family, specialises in French food and also has three stars.

The 13th-century church of St Michael has some interesting old carvings from its predecessor, which was built some distance away from the village. There is a famous satirical 18th-century song called 'The Vicar of Bray', and the now defunct Bray Studios produced over 80 Hammer horror films in the 1950s and 1960s, as well as further cinematic blockbusters as recently as 2000.

9 **Dorney Lakes** Part of the Eton College Rowing Centre, Dorney Lakes is a modern world-class rowing and flat-water canoeing centre on the banks of the Thames. It is scheduled to host the rowing, flat-water and slalom canoeing and kayaking events during the London Olympics in 2012. Part of a 450-acre parkland, it frequently hosts corporate and private events.

10 **Boveney** The lovely little chapel of St Mary Magdalene sits in solitude on the banks of the river. Its rubble chalk courses are well buttressed and crowned with a clapboard belfry, sitting at a rakish angle. The earliest parts date from the 12th and 13th centuries and it probably served a wharf here, shipping timber from Windsor Forest. Boveney hamlet itself, just up the path beyond the chapel, has several well-restored timber-framed Tudor houses.

11 **Athens Bathing Site** Along the towpath here you will pass a featureless platform with a bench and a low tablet, which tells you that this, believe it or not, is Athens, traditional bathing place for the boys from Eton. Quoting from the rules: 'boys who are undressed must either get at once into the water or get behind screens when boats containing ladies come in sight'.

Marlow

The fine riverside town of Marlow has a long and fascinating history. Its development is due to its strategic location on the River Thames between Reading and High Wycombe.

The town is graced by a beautiful suspension bridge over the Thames, designed by William Tierney Clark and completed in 1832 (see Bridges, page 19). Its design resembles Hammersmith Bridge, which you will pass later on your Thames Path walk, and also a bridge over the River Danube in Budapest. On the bridge causeway you will see a statue to the theatrical impresario Charles Frohman, who went down with the *Lusitania* in 1915.

From the bridge it is only a short distance to All Saints Church with its elegant, pinnacled spire. The combination of church and bridge have forged one of the most famous compositions along the River Thames. There has probably been a place of worship on this site since Anglo Saxon times, but the current church was rebuilt in 1835. In the churchyard can be seen the grave of the 'Spotted Boy' – a young slave from the Caribbean with unusual colouring who was taken round the country on show and died at the age of four.

St Peter's Church, nearby, was designed by Augustus Pugin in 1848 and is said to house the mummified hand of the Apostle St James, who was present at the Last Supper.

There are many fine Georgian buildings in the town centre, some with distinguished literary associations. The poet Percy Bysshe Shelley and his wife Mary stayed in the town from 1817–18 and it was here that Mary Shelley completed her novel *Frankenstein*. Another poet, T. S. Eliot, lived here in the early 20th century, and the town features prominently in Jerome K. Jerome's classic *Three Men in a Boat*.

A large mansion called Court Garden stands in the town's Higginson Park. The house was designed and built by a Dr Battie, who specialised in nervous diseases, and it is said that initially he forgot to include a staircase. The park, which is conveniently located next to the Thames Path, is named after a Crimean War veteran, Sir George Higginson, in celebration of his 100th birthday. The Marlow Museum is located adjacent to the house and is well worth a visit.

Excellent road connections mean that today Marlow has become a bustling commuter town. Its rail connections are a bit more eccentric. The exact reason is unclear, but the railway link from Maidenhead to Marlow on a single-track branch line has become affectionately known as the Marlow Donkey.

The pinnacled church tower and the lines of the suspension bridge at Marlow create an eye-catching composition.

Detail of The Resurrection, Cookham, *painted by Stanley Spencer in 1924–7.*

Cookham

With its railway connections to London, Cookham is a thriving, affluent community with a good range of restaurants and pubs. It has a fascinating history and its most famous resident was the renowned English artist Sir Stanley Spencer.

He was born in Cookham in 1891 in a house called Fernlea. He was one of 11 children and as a boy was very small for his age. He loved Cookham and the surrounding area all his life, calling it his 'village in heaven'. At the age of 17 he went to the Slade School of Art in London, where his talents were soon noted by the tutors. While at the Slade he earned himself the nickname 'Cookham' because he talked so much about the village and returned home there every night.

Stanley Spencer was called up in the First World War and served on the Western Front and in Greece. During the Second World War he was commissioned as a war artist and painted shipyards on the Clyde in Scotland.

He was a prolific painter and throughout his life spent as much time as he could in Cookham. His paintings of local scenes include *Swan Upping at Cookham*, *View from Cookham Bridge* and *Bellrope Meadow*. He was particularly fascinated by the churchyard and portrayed it in many of his works. His painting *The Resurrection, Cookham* shows Spencer and his friends rising sleepily from the graves you see from the Thames Path as it passes through Cookham churchyard. Spencer was knighted in 1959 but died later that year and his ashes lie in the churchyard.

You can learn more about this remarkable man by visiting the Stanley Spencer Gallery, a small but fascinating building which was formerly a Wesleyan Chapel. It opened in 1962, and claims to be the only gallery in Britain devoted exclusively to an artist in the village where he was born and spent his working life.

Cookham has further cultural connections, as Kenneth Grahame, author of *The Wind in the Willows*, grew up here.

On your walk through the village you may well notice a large sarsen stone, known as the Tarry Stone, which was placed in its current location in 1909. Its history is the subject of much speculation.

Marlow to Windsor

Route description

From **Marlow** **1** Bridge down to the lock, there is no towpath, and barges had to be manhandled or hauled on a long towline while their towing horses were led round on a tortuous path. So, keeping to the tradition, the Thames Path sets off along that odd route, known locally as Seven Corner Alley, for reasons that will soon be obvious. Retrace your steps to the bridge and follow a Thames Path sign on the north side of All Saints Church. Then cross the corner of the churchyard **A** to emerge in St Peter Street opposite the charming 🍺 Two Brewers pub.

A few paces to the right, the path continues, bending this way and that between high walls to reach another road where you turn right to the riverside.

Although your route now follows the road for a while, it is well worth turning aside briefly on the path to the right, signed to Marlow Lock, to enjoy the classic view of church and bridge over the weir. Downstream, you cannot miss the striking, angular roofs of the weatherboarded housing on the site of Marlow Mill, its mill-like ambience still retained.

Walking on along the road, you pass the mill housing, then, around a left-hand bend, a gravel path to the right leads through a small park to the Thames **B**, where it turns left to go to the river side of houses and then under the bypass bridge. Now the great, beech-clad rise of Quarry Wood blocks the way, and the Thames turns aside to skirt the foot of Winter Hill. There are boathouses by the

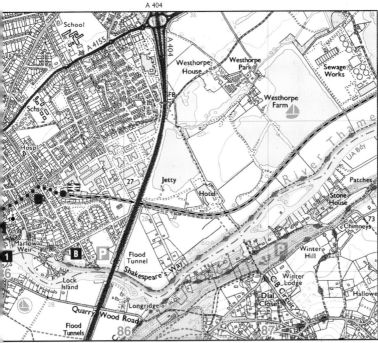

...rs are given in metres   A 404
...rtical interval is 5m

Look out for the Stanley Spencer memorial stone as you pass through the churchyard of Holy Trinity in Cookham.

waterside and villas climbing the slopes. One property on the bank is a genuine mini-castle with turrets and battlements, a cheeky but perfect complement to its dramatic river setting. As you come on to grass, a magnificent poplar avenue screens playing fields, and picnic benches invite you to linger. Then over a footbridge and through several kissing-gates, you are into open meadows, with the slopes of Winter Hill, bare now, falling back from the river. On the opposite side, the very last white cottage is Spade Oak Ferry Cottage, yet another old towpath crossing.

Off to the left, a level crossing over the little branch line leads past the spruced-up Spade Oak Farm and, just around the bend, the Spade Oak pub.

Your way continues on a broad track just back from the Thames. Bourne End ahead is a favourite reach for dinghy sailing. White gates lead you on to a paved path across the Upper Thames Sailing Club lawn and on past the handsome clubhouse. Then come moored motor cruisers and a gravel walkway past housing, leading to a bridge over a small marina with a restaurant over its office. Briefly you join a road, but where it turns away left towards **Bourne End 2**, a narrow path next to Dinnies Riverside Open Space continues ahead between garden fences towards the railway bridge.

An old metal gate on your right leads to a footbridge attached to the railway bridge **C**.

For Bourne End station, go under the railway bridge and turn immediately left on a path to the station car park.

Cross the footbridge and walk under the railway bridge, then go through a wooden kissing-gate into the National Trust-owned **Cock Marsh 3**.

To visit The Bounty pub on Cock Marsh, walk a short distance back upstream towards Marlow and the pub lies ahead on the towpath.

Your path keeps to the river bank through the open meadows via several kissing-gates until a bend brings Cookham Bridge into view. Go through some more gates and walk across the Cookham Reach Sailing Club area into Bellrope Meadow public open space on a surfaced path. When the tidy grass ends, just short of the bridge, turn right into Cookham churchyard **D** through an old metal kissing-gate. The path goes to the right of the sturdy 16th-century tower of Holy Trinity, and on through the old gravestones to a group of white buildings beyond. This is Churchgate, where you bear left, then right on the main road to the village centre.

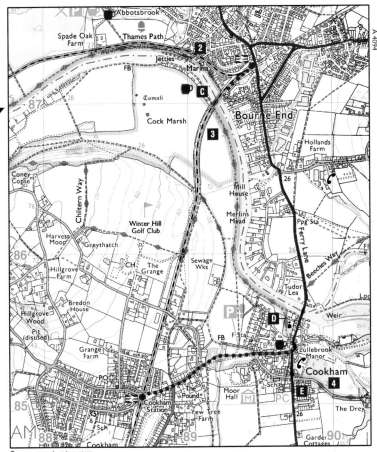

Contours are given in metres
The vertical interval is 5m

On a corner across the road you can see the Tarry Stone, a big chunk of sarsen stone and the subject of many local tales.

🏠☕🚤 *The next turning to the right leads up Cookham High Street, past the Bel and the Dragon Inn and the Kings Arms, out on to the open common, Cookham Moor. For the station, cross the Moor and go straight on through the newer houses of Cookham Rise.*

Facing you is the Wesleyan chapel, re-opened in 1962 as a memorial gallery for the work of Stanley Spencer, the artist who immortalised **Cookham 4**

and drew a lifetime's inspiration from the village and its people.

Just below Cookham Bridge the Thames blossoms into no fewer than four channels, two of which enclose Formosa Island. Three ferries were needed to get the towpath past all this, so understandably you have a diversion away from the river here. Continue ahead along Sutton Road, passing the Stanley Spencer gallery on the right, and turning left after 200 yards (180 metres) down Mill Lane **E**, which passes through open fields. Arriving at houses again, the path goes right between hedges, curves round a property, crosses a drive, then continues as a woodland way with open fields just to the right. Keep by the field edge around several bends until the path, with a touch of drama, suddenly comes to the river bank at 'My Lady Ferry', an old ferry crossing point. Across the river, the beechwoods rise steeply. At your feet are the last traces of the ferry landing and, opposite, the elegant estate cottages and well-tended lawns of the Cliveden Estate. This reach can be magnificent in autumn, the hanging woods reflecting in the water to create a sheer wall of colour.

Walk on a little and you should be able to look back to **Cliveden 5** itself – commanding on its hilltop platform. The path, narrow in places, continues ahead, tree-lined and fenced, passing occasional islets in the river. Approaching **Boulter's Lock 6**, with thundering water across the Thames, civilisation returns to the near bank in the shape of lawns, landing stages and smart cruisers at their moorings. Follow the lock cut up to the road, then continue along the pavement to Boulter's Lock itself. By the lock, a bridge leads over to Ray Mill Island, 4 acres (1.6 hectares) of public garden, and to the hotel, which was once a flour mill.

Continue along the promenade beside the river and a little before Maidenhead bridge there is ➤ Jenners Riverside Café on your right in a small public garden. Approaching Maidenhead Bridge, keep on the promenade and pass behind some riverside flats before emerging back on the main road. Take the path through Bridge Gardens to the bridge itself.

▢➤⇄🚌 *To visit* **Maidenhead 7** *town centre, turn right up Bridge Road, the A4. For Maidenhead station and buses, also turn right up Bridge Road. At a big roundabout, turn left into Forlease Road, then second right into York Road, at the end of which bear left along Queen Street to the station. The bus stops are down the first turning on the right off York Road.*

To continue on the Thames Path, cross Maidenhead Bridge by the upstream pavement, turn left on the other side and immediately left again through gates into a boatyard **F**. Go through another gate and under an arch of the bridge and along the concrete wharf past Maidenhead Rowing Club on the other side. Beyond a boathouse development, turn up through a car park to River Road and follow it, to the right, towards Isambard Kingdom Brunel's masterpiece of a railway bridge, designed in 1839 to carry his broad-gauge line to the West Country.

Autumn begins to colour the hanging woods of the Cliveden estate.

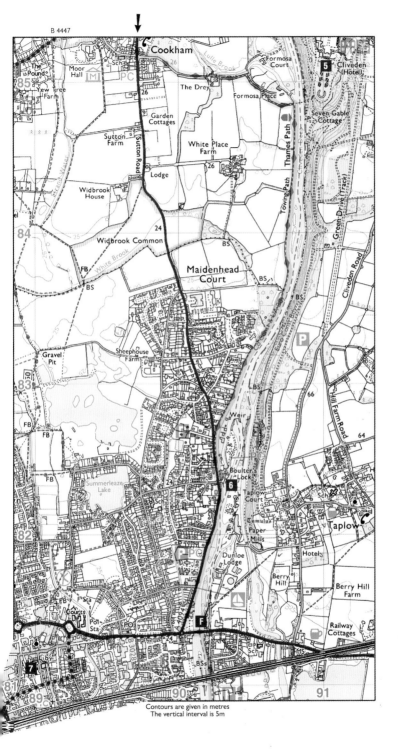

Contours are given in metres
The vertical interval is 5m

Beyond the bridge, you are on a riverside road for a while, then, when it turns away, your tree-lined footpath continues, green and pleasant, towards Bray Lock. The tower of the church and then the village of **Bray 8** itself appears over the river. Go straight through Bray Lock and the access road to return to the towpath. The sound of thundering traffic ahead indicates that the M4 motorway crosses the river ahead and you soon pass under the bridge. For a while, the path is well preserved through gates and across the grass at the bottom of some large gardens. Now you come to a footbridge over the Thames that also carries a cycle route. Summerleaze Bridge opened in 1996 and supported a conveyor belt carrying gravel from the excavation of the Eton College rowing site – **Dorney Lakes 9** – on your left, which is the venue for rowing and kayak events in the 2012 Olympic Games. Do not cross it, but continue, soon reaching the great open field of Dorney, Thames Field.

At the time of writing, the Thames Path has been temporarily diverted here away from the river bank and around the back of the Dorney Lakes, as a 2-mile (3.2-km) stretch of the towpath may be closed until November 2012 due to works connected with the London Olympics. Please follow signs. The temporary route, which follows National Cycle Route 4, passes to the north of the lake complex to re-emerge on the Thames Path at Boveney.

The Thames Path winds along the river bank near Bray Lock, in the Dorney area.

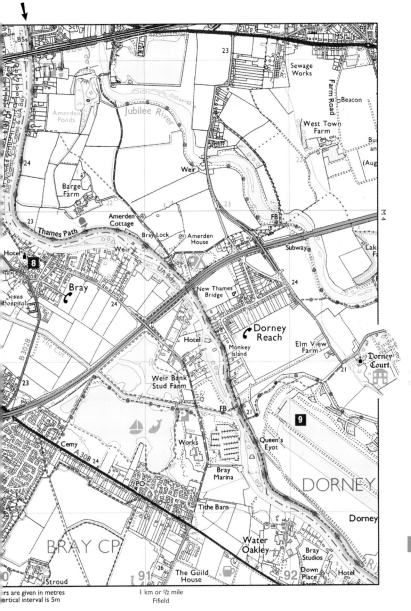

rs are given in metres
ertical interval is 5m

1 km or 1/2 mile
Fifield

The official route continues ahead on the towpath. The path to the left offers a tempting diversion to the delectable grouping of Tudor Dorney Court and the church of St James, hiding peacefully together near the river. To

the left are views across Dorney Lake Country Park and the main rowing lake itself. Across the river is Oakley Court, high Victorian Gothic with towers and fanciful animals crouching on the roofs. With a puff of dry ice it could well serve

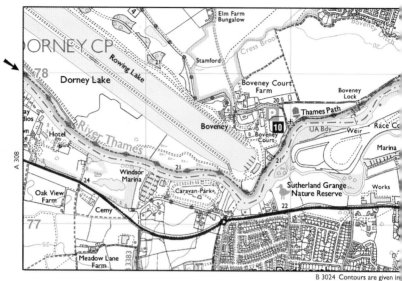

B 3024 Contours are given in
The vertical interval

as Dracula's Castle, and indeed probably has. Around another bend, past a college boathouse, the simple little chapel of St Mary Magdalene, **Boveney** 🔟, stands in solitude by the river.

Your way is on now on the towpath through Boveney Lock, with the houses of Eton Wick across the expanse of South Field to the left, and Windsor Racecourse across the river. Passing the **Athens Bathing Site** 🔟 and over a small footbridge, the path goes through open meadowland around a river loop. Then it continues under a road bridge and a railway bridge, its long viaduct bringing the line along from Slough. You then enter an open space known as the Brocas meadow, named after a local family. Now you can see Windsor Castle in all its majesty towering over the town.

Leave the Brocas by a gate 🄶 to the left of a white house on the riverside, go to the right of the 🍺 Waterman's Arms and out to the foot of the narrow and decidedly picturesque Eton High Street.

🚏🚤 *To explore the interesting shops and famous Eton College buildings, turn left here up the High Street. Eton can also be explored as part of the walking tour of Windsor and Eton – a see page 145.*

The Thames Path goes right at the High Street to cross over the pedestrians-only bridge into Windsor.

Windsor is very well served with railway transport, as rival companies competed for royal patronage and, as a result, the town gained two substantial train stations.

🚆 *For Windsor and Eton Riverside station, go down the steps on the left over the bridge, walk along the riverside for 70 yard (64 metres) and turn right. For Central station, walk ahead from the bridge and bear right with Thames Street beneath the castle ramparts. The grand station entry is down a turning on the right just beyond the castle entrance.* The Visitor Information Centre is located nearby in the Old Booking Office in the Royal Windsor shopping Centre on Thames Street.

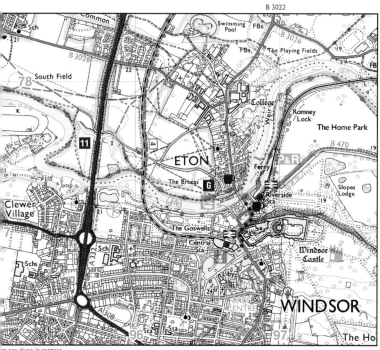

B 3022

rs are given in metres
rtical interval is 5m

Public transport

Bourne End (on route) ⇌ 🚌
Cookham Rise (1 mile/1.6 km) ⇌
Maidenhead (on route) ⇌ 🚌
Windsor (on route) ⇌ 🚌

Refreshments and toilets

Well End (0.2 mile/0.3 km) 🍴 Spade Oak
Cock Marsh (0.2 mile/0.3 km) 🍴
The Bounty (limited winter opening times)
Bourne End (0.3 mile/0.5 km) 🍴 Walnut
Tree, The Firefly, The Garibaldi, Black Lion
Cookham (on route) 🍴 Kings Arms, The
Ferry, The Crown; ☕ Station Hill Good
Food Café
Maidenhead (on route) 🍴☕ wide
selection
Eton (on route) 🍴☕ wide selection
Windsor (on route) 🍴☕ wide selection
Food shops: Marlow, Bourne End,
Cookham, Maidenhead, Eton, Windsor

Public toilets: Marlow, Marlow Lock,
Bourne End, Cookham, Maidenhead, Bray
Lock, Boveney Lock, Eton, Windsor

Accommodation

Cookham Dean (2 miles/3.2 km)
Cartlands Cottage, Sanctum on the Green
Bourne End (0.3 mile/0.5 km) Hollands
Farm, Old Cottage
Cookham (on route) Swiss B&B,
The Crown
Maidenhead (on route) wide selection –
contact Visitor Information Centre
Taplow (1.1 miles/1.8 km) Cliveden,
Amerden Lodge, Bridge Cottage, Amerden
campsite
Bray (1.3 miles/2 km) Old Coach House
Eton (on route) The Christopher, Crown and
Cushion
Windsor (on route) wide selection –
contact Visitor Information Centre

Windsor to Shepperton

via Datchet, Runnymede, Staines and Chertsey
13¾ miles (22.1 km)

Although this varied section of the trail brings us into Greater London, with an inevitable increase in development along the river bank, it passes places of great historic interest and superbly highlights the importance played by the Thames in the development of the country. It starts in Royal Windsor and this chapter includes a separate walking tour of Windsor and neighbouring Eton, as there is so much history to be discovered in both these fascinating places – see page 145. From Windsor and its parklands you pass through the meadows of Runnymede, where events of national and international significance took place in 1215. Entering Greater London under the M25, the busy and developed riverside through Staines and Laleham jolts you back into the modern world. The open flood meadows around Chertsey Bridge are a final reminder of the rural river before you arrive at the ferry near Shepperton Lock. Surprisingly, you may be accompanied overhead by the shrill cries of parakeets, looking somewhat out of place away from their more tropical natural habitats.

Transport options

From Windsor, a 2-mile (3.2-km) stroll brings you to Datchet; then it's a further 6¼ miles (10 km) to Staines. Both points have convenient connections on the same railway line that serves Windsor and Eton Riverside Stations. From Staines it is another 5½-mile (8.8-km) walk on to Shepperton, where there are rail connections to London Waterloo.

Things to look out for

1 Datchet A fascinating riverside village with a long history linking it to Windsor. There is an interesting story behind the old Datchet Bridge, which was demolished in the 1850s, when two new bridges – Victoria and Albert – were built to create a private riverside park for Queen Victoria. No trace of the old bridge remains, but by all accounts it was a strange affair. The boundary between Berkshire and Buckinghamshire ran through the centre of the span and when, in the 1830s, urgent repairs were needed, Berks rebuilt their half in iron while Bucks merely repaired theirs – in wood. The two halves didn't touch in the middle and the

structure was known as 'the Divided Bridge'. It is the only Thames crossing point that has lost its bridge.

Datchet was home in the 1780s to the famous astronomer Sir William Herschel, and in the early 20th century to Tommy Sopwith, the pioneering aviator. In 1895 it became the first place in Britain to witness the arrival of the motor car. The railway and excellent road connections have turned Datchet today into a modern commuter village.

2 Old Windsor This large village to the south of Windsor was the oldest Saxon town in Berkshire and the seat of Edward the Confessor, but its importance has dwindled with the emergence of Windsor itself. In the past Old Windsor was popular with the monarchy due to its river links and convenience for hunting in Windsor Forest. The 13th-century church of St Peter and St Andrew is a short way from the Thames Path down a footpath.

3 Runnymede Nearly 800 years ago events that shaped our nation took place in this National Trust-owned meadow to the west of the Thames. Somewhere in this area in 1215 King John set his seal on the Magna Carta (the 'Great Charter'), though the precise location is unknown. This document, which was a formal acceptance of the demands of the barons, liberated the population from the power of absolute monarchy. Subsequently this became enshrined in English Law and formed the bedrock of national constitutions around the English-speaking world.

Runnymede has three memorials to visit. First, in 1953 the Air Force Memorial was unveiled by the Queen. Designed by Sir Edward Maufe, it commemorates the 20,456 airmen who lost their lives in the Second World War and have no known grave. It sits high on the skyline above Runnymede and offers far-reaching views across seven counties. The other two memorials are closer to the Thames Path. In 1957 a domed classical temple, the Magna Carta Memorial, was built at the foot of Cooper's Hill. Again designed by Maufe, it was funded by US lawyers and built by the American Bar Association. In 1965 a John F. Kennedy Memorial was unveiled on land that has been given to the USA in perpetuity. Designed by G. A. Jellicoe in Portland stone, it is a memorial to liberty and nationhood.

The two memorial gatehouses at the road entrance to Runnymede were designed by Sir Edward Lutyens and commissioned by Lady Fairhaven. They form a memorial to her husband, Sir Urban Broughton MP, who bought Runnymede in 1928 to safeguard its future. One houses a popular tea room.

Magna Carta Island in the Thames conceals the scant traces of the 12th-century nunnery of Ankerwycke, which was a possible site for the signing of the famous charter (see Islands, page 22).

A traditional Thames sight: swans crowd the river near Windsor Bridge.

When passing through Runnymede, try to ignore the picnic parties and the traffic, and respond instead to the ambience of those great historic moments which still lingers in these meadows by the Thames.

4 Staines This large Thames town has a long history. It has been a river crossing point since Roman times and the barons gathered in this area in 1215 before meeting King John at Runnymede. Sir Thomas More was tried here in a public house in 1535 to avoid the plague that was affecting London at the time. A stone commemorates the fact that Staines was a horse-change site in 1805 when news was being delivered about the death of Horatio Nelson. The town has developed due to its proximity to London and was a major producer of linoleum. The old town hall, in Italianate style, sits in attractive riverside surroundings.

5 Penton Hook This is surely the most impressive river loop along the whole Thames. Early in the 19th century its narrow neck was broken through by flood waters so regularly that barges took a 'short-cut'. The first lock was built here in 1815 in recognition of this, and today the island, managed by the Environment Agency, has the feel of a nature reserve. It was built up with spoil from dredging, but has now been reclaimed by ash, hawthorn and elder, and presents a fine, wild aspect. If you have time, cross either of the lock gates and the main weir beyond, and try the paths around the island. Popular with anglers, it is a wildlife haven in a relatively urbanised area.

6 Laleham A riverside village with a particularly rich and diverse history. There is thought to have been a 1st-century Roman marching camp in a field in the village and Iron Age spearheads have been found on the banks of the Thames at Laleham Ferry. All Saints Church dates from the 12th century and monks from Westminster operated a grange and watermill here in the 13th century. The village has many ancient and historic buildings, the best known of which is Laleham House (also called Laleham Abbey), the seat of the Lucan family. It was the 7th Earl of Lucan who famously disappeared in 1974 after being accused of murdering the family nanny at their London home. When the Lucans departed, the house was divided up into flats and the 70 acres of grounds were given to the public as Laleham Park.

The poet Matthew Arnold, who wrote about the Thames at Bablock Hythe in *The Scholar Gipsy*, was born in Laleham and is buried in All Saints Churchyard.

7 Chertsey With its proximity to the M3 and good transport links to London, Chertsey has become a large commuter town. It has an extremely long and fascinating history, being one of the oldest recorded towns in the country. It was built up around Chertsey Abbey, founded by the Bishop of London in AD 666, which grew to become one of the largest Benedictine abbeys in the country until its dissolution by Henry VIII in 1536. The present seven-arch stone Chertsey Bridge dates from 1783–5 and replaced an earlier timber construction. Chertsey Museum has many interesting artefacts and stories about the long history of the town.

On the Middlesex, or eastern, side of the bridge is Dumsey Meadow, one of the few remaining traditional watermeadows on the River Thames and home to a variety of plants and insects.

A Circular Walk around Windsor and Eton

Starts and finishes on the pedestrianised Windsor Bridge linking Windsor and Eton over the Thames

3 miles (4.8 km); Long Walk 5¼ miles (8.3 km); total distance 8¼ miles (13 km)

Turn away from Windsor, heading north over the bridge and straight along Eton High Street. This historic street is lined with magnificent ancient buildings. Just on the right after passing King Stable Street (where once the king's horses were stabled) you will pass the Tiger Garden Restaurant. This wonderful old building, formerly known as the Cockpit Restaurant, was built in 1420. Live cockfights used to take place at the back of the building and the old cockpit can still be seen. Note the unusual vertical slot for letters on the earliest Victorian postbox in the country, which is just on the right.

Further up the High Street are the grand building of Coutts Bank and two traditional school outfitters to Eton College – **Billings & Edmonds** and **Tom Brown Tailors**. Tom Brown have been at the same address on Eton High Street since 1784.

Cross a bridge and the grand buildings of **Eton College** form an impressive sight on the right. First comes the magnificent **Eton College Chapel**, a wonderful example of 14th-century Perpendicular Gothic architecture, followed by the main college buildings. The college entrance is to the right now, while we turn left into Common Lane. Look out for the Russian gun that was captured at Sevastopol in 1855 in the forecourt of the Geography Department.

Eton College was founded by Henry VI in 1440 and has become one of the most famous public schools in the world. It has produced an endless line of outstanding scholars and David Cameron is the 19th prime minister to have been educated at Eton.

Continue down Common Lane, passing Eton College houses and halls of residence. Keep ahead until you pass the swimming-pool complex on the right and a vast railway viaduct appears ahead. Just before the viaduct turn left down a track alongside the railway, which is also a cycle route. Note the huge number of arches on the viaduct – this is one of the longest railway viaducts in the country. Keep ahead to meet the busy B3026 to Eton Wick. Here turn left slightly and cross the road to continue in the same direction, with a fence and the viaduct on your right. You are now on National Cycle Route 4, with good views towards Eton College and Windsor Castle.

The statue of Queen Victoria guards the imposing towers of Windsor Castle.

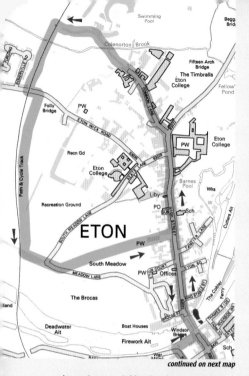

ETON

continued on next map

This area directly in front of the castle is always busy with tourists, as the public entrance is nearby.

Windsor Castle is the oldest and largest continually occupied castle in the world. Established by William the Conqueror in the 11th century, it has been enlarged and improved by successive monarchs. Nearly demolished in the Civil War and disastrously damaged by fire in 1992, Windsor Castle has come to symbolise British history and is the Queen's favourite weekend retreat.

Keep walking ahead along Windsor High Street. The best-preserved of the narrow streets and ancient buildings which make up the historic central core of Windsor are on your left now. First you will pass the end of **Queen Charlotte Street** – at 51 feet 10 inches long it is one the shortest streets in the country. Next comes the Crooked House Tea Room, which was originally built in 1592 but rebuilt in 1687 using unseasoned oak, with unfortunate consequences! It is squeezed in beside the Sir Christopher Wren-designed **Guildhall**, the official town hall of Windsor, which was built between 1687 and 1689.

If you have time, it is worth exploring more fully the tight group of streets of the old town around Church Street, Church Hill and Market Street. These narrow, cobbled streets may be full of restaurants and shops, but they also contain a wealth of history. Note the copy of the death warrant for King Charles I in 1648 on the wall of Ye Olde Kings Head pub, where Shakespeare may have written *The Merry Wives of Windsor*.

Back on the High Street, keep ahead past the church of **St John the Baptist**, which dates from 1822. It replaced an ancient building with Saxon arches and Norman work. It is well worth a visit and contains a superb and vast painting of the Last Supper. At the next junction turn half-left into Park Street. Note the ancient well and the blue letterbox on the left commemorating the first airmail service, introduced in 1911 for George V's coronation. Park Street was once a major stagecoach route to and from London, and is lined with

At a minor road, Meadow Lane, turn left and walk as far as the next road junction. Here take the footpath between the hedges to the left that leads across the open playing fields directly towards Eton Church tower. Aim for the alleyway to the left of the church and note some of its other uses as you pass by. As well as a church, it is also a medical centre, Eton College sanatorium and flats for college staff. Walk on through the Eton War Memorial Garden to emerge once again on Eton High Street. Turn right and retrace your steps back to the Windsor Bridge.

Cross the bridge and keep ahead at the next junction to climb up and to the right along Thames Street, with the vast bulk of **Windsor Castle** looming overhead. You pass the Theatre Royal as the road bends left to become the High Street. The entrance to the Windsor Royal Shopping Centre and the Tourist Information Centre in the refurbished Victorian central railway station is on your right. Look for the fine bronze **statue of Queen Victoria** at the junction with Castle Hill – it was unveiled in 1887 to commemorate the Queen's golden jubilee.

elegant Georgian mansions. The attractive Two Brewers Pub is conveniently located as you go ahead through the Cambridge Park gates into Windsor Home Park.

At the castle gates turn half-right to look along the famous **Long Walk** towards a mound and statue just visible in the far distance. The Long Walk extends for 2.6 miles (4.1 km) and makes for easy walking in a straight line from Windsor Castle to **Snow Hill**. The statue on Snow Hill, known as the Copper Horse, dates from 1829 and is of King George III on horseback; it marks the end of this walk. If you do wish to venture further, the Long Walk is at the start of a long-distance walking route, the Three Castles Path, a 60-mile (96-km) trail which starts at Windsor Castle and continues south-westwards via the recently restored Odiham Castle to Winchester Castle Hall in Hampshire.

Take care crossing the busy A308 road and pass through the gates into the **Windsor Great Park** deer park. You can enjoy good views back to the castle all along this walk, and you can reduce the distance by turning back at any stage but, to get a wonderful panorama of Windsor Castle, the buildings of Eton College and the Thames Valley, walking the full distance to the statue on the hill is strongly recommended. The route is clear and straight ahead on the wide track, until very close to the statue you meet a cross-path that's popular with cyclists. Cross this path and scramble up the grassy mound to the summit to enjoy the wonderful views all around.

The return journey is straightforward, as you simply retrace your steps back along the Long Walk, through the deer park gates and over the A308 towards the castle. Soon after seeing the Windsor Castle pub on the road to the left of the park, a path turns diagonally towards the left, arriving at the Brook Street gates. Walk through the gates to the end of Brook Street and turn left then straight right into Francis Street. Turn immediately right into Keppel Street, which winds around the walls of the huge Victoria Barracks.

You are now amongst the suburban houses of Windsor. Keep ahead at the end of Keppel Street, which turns into Helena Street and follow this to the end by the Prince Arthur pub. Turn right into Grove Road with its attractive housing and follow it as far as the shop-lined St Leonard's Road. On the left here is the old fire station, now a successful arts centre. Turn right up along the shops of St Leonard's Road and keep ahead into the pedestrianised Peascod Street with great views ahead towards Windsor Castle. Peascod Street is one of the oldest streets in Windsor, named after an area where peas were grown – a staple diet in medieval times.

At the end of this road you again meet the High Street near the Queen Victoria statue. Turn left along Thames Street, this time turning left into River Street, where you walk towards the river. When the road turns left, keep ahead to the riverside. Turn right and the towpath will take you back to Windsor Bridge and the end of the walk.

continued from previous map

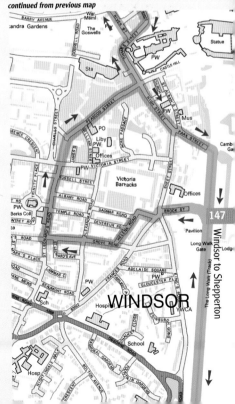

WINDSOR

147

Windsor to Shepperton

The Long Walk Trail

Route description

From Windsor Bridge take the steps down to the riverside promenade on the downstream, Windsor, side, and walk past Salter's office, where their riverboats, which offer trips to Runnymede and Staines, are often moored. Ahead, a narrow spit of land called The Cobbler separates weir stream from lock cut, carrying a section of the old towpath that ends rather forlornly in midstream. Just beyond 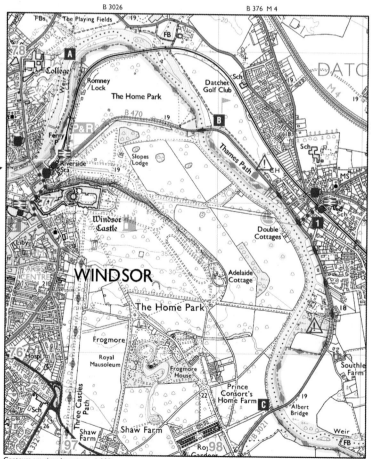 the River House, go ahead through gates on to Romney Walk with railings on both sides. Soon you are bearing left along a broader drive that leads to Romney Lock. Go to the right of the red-brick tower of the Victorian waterworks and enter a boatyard. Your route is mostly fenced off from the working area and heads left towards a footbridge leading to the lock. Bear right before you reach it, to a large wooden kissing-gate **A** into open fields. Walk on with the lock cut still to your left, then under Black Potts railway bridge and out into the open

Contours are given in metres   A 308
The vertical interval is 5m

e is scarcely a ripple to disturb this
quil scene in Home Park near Windsor.

area of the Home Park. Windsor Castle, beyond the playing fields, provides the distant backdrop.

Before you now is Victoria Bridge. The towpath ahead is closed for security reasons, so your path changes to the other bank. First, bear right over the grass to a point where the white railings of the bridge approach the road end. Cross the road here and go left over Victoria Bridge on the downstream pavement. Once over the river, go down a steep flight of steps **B** and follow the path, a lovely woodland stretch, until it leads away from the river and back towards the road. As there is no footway on the near side, cross the road with care and turn right towards Datchet **1**.

🚶 *For Datchet village centre, take either of the two road turnings left.*

🚆 *For Datchet railway station, take the second turning left, the High Street, which passes the station.*

Follow the road through Datchet until, just beyond the last riverside properties, you can cross carefully at a Thames Path fingerpost to a short plank footbridge opposite. Once over it, a fenced path follows the road, then turns right away from the road to the river bank. Walk under Albert Bridge, up the slope through a kissing-gate to cross the bridge and turn down the steep concrete steps **C** to rejoin the towpath. The path here is narrow in parts and slippery in the wet. Soon the true channel of the Thames turns away to the left, but you must continue along a lock cut on a path that joins the drive to Old Windsor Lock. Follow the road through the lock and half a mile (800

The American Bar Society's Magna Carta Memorial at Runnymede reminds us that events of world significance happened in these Thames meadows.

metres) further on you pass a small marina by a footbridge.

*To visit the church of St Peter and St Andrew in **Old Windsor** 2, follow the footpath to the right.*

The path continues between river and road with properties on both sides of the river, eventually coming out to the roadside.

▱ *The bustling Bells of Ouzeley is located just over the busy A308 to the right.*

After passing a busy road junction, keep ahead and soon the path **D** leaves the road to the left to follow the river past the French Brothers boat landing and out into the meadows of **Runnymede** 3.

Immediately to the right here are two of the Lutyens gatehouses; the one across the road houses the popular ☕ Magna Carta Tea Room, with toilets nearby. Just ahead of you, a display panel by a car park entry locates the Runnymede memorials.

Halfway along the Runnymede meadow, be careful not to follow the riverside too closely into a 'dead end' spit of land, but be guided by waymark posts nearer the road. Across the Thames are the wooded banks of Magna Carta Island.

As the river curves to the left, leave Runnymede by passing through a gap in the fence. Ahead, near the roadside, is the 🍵 Runnymede Pleasure Grounds Café and more toilets, but the Thames Path, now on grass and keeping close by the river bank, heads for Staines. Going past Wraysbury Skiff and Rowing Club, you pass charming bungalows – their tubs and flowerbeds a glory of well-tended colour in summer – and occasional small boatyards.

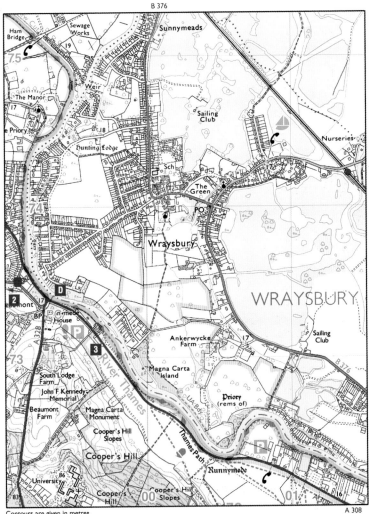

Contours are given in metres
The vertical interval is 5m

Pass Bellweir Lock and the vast new Runnymede-on-Thames Hotel and carry on under the double motorway bridge. To many, it is the thunder of M25 traffic overhead that carries the sure message that you are entering London. But there are other clues to a boundary crossing nearby. A short way on, as you pass a superstore car park, you may spot a white iron post by the towpath. This is a 'coal post', one of many that ringed the entries to London to warn merchants that, under an Act of 1831, they were now due to pay a levy on coal. And, almost hidden by trees on the far bank, there is a replica of the London Stone, placed here to mark the upstream limit of the City of London's jurisdiction over the Thames, which lasted from 1285 to 1857, when the first Thames Conservators took over.

Ahead, over a large footbridge, you arrive at Staines Bridge.

📖 Under it the towpath leads to the Hythe, a little Thames-side community with some pleasant cottages and pubs ('hythe' means a landing place).

The Thames Path, however, turns right up the slope to cross Staines Bridge on the upstream pavement, then continues down the steps on the other bank to a car park area.

📖 🍽 The town centre of **Staines** 4 is just to the north of the river at this point.

Walk back beside the bridge to rejoin the Thames and turn under Staines Bridge to walk downstream again. Cross the River Colne on a footbridge, then, coming to a small garden with fountains, spare a minute to divert up a path on the left to the little market square with its pretty town hall.

The river walk continues until, where the garden promenade ends, the Thames Path joins the road and turns

The Swan Hotel at Staines.

FULLER'S

THE SWAN HOTEL

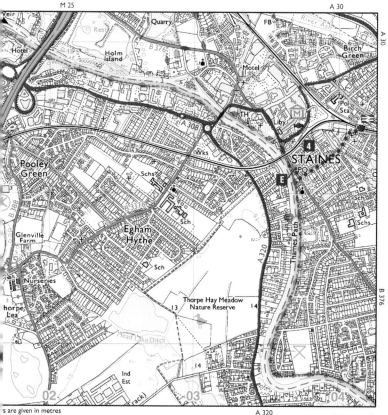

s are given in metres
tical interval is 5m   A 320

right. But during daylight hours you can continue through gates here, and along the river front of the Thames Lodge Hotel. By either route, right beneath Staines railway bridge you find the start of the towpath again. The stone slipway here was the 'shut-off' point at which horse teams were detached and led up to Staines Bridge, from where the towline was floated down to pick up the barge.

From Staines railway bridge, the towpath continues as a broad, metalled path past riverside houses **E**.

≋ *For Staines station, keep on along the road and take the third turning on the left, Gresham Road; the footbridge at the top takes you into the station yard.*

Along riverside Staines, the little houses, in their infinite variety, still reflect the joy of simply living by the Thames. Too many have recently given way to out-of-scale apartment blocks, but the affection still felt by locals for their riverside is evident in the number of dedicated seats along it; 'Cli and John welcome you' is the message on one little two-seater.

For a short distance you will take paths over an open grass area before a broad, gravel track leads on past more

Windsor to Shepperton

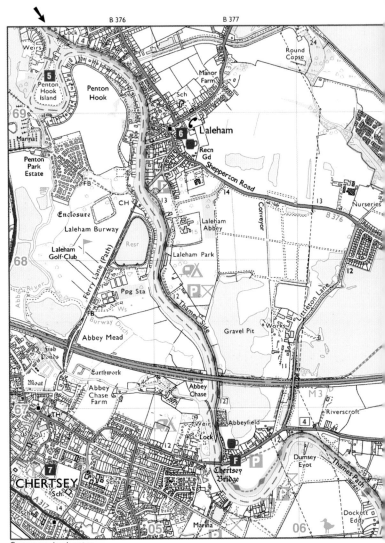

B 376

B 377

Contours are given in metres
The vertical interval is 5m

properties to Penton Hook Lock. Beyond **Penton Hook 5**, now on a road, you cross the intake to Thames Water's vast Queen Mary Reservoir.

🔲 *Turn left up Blacksmiths' Lane to reach the centre of **Laleham** 6 and, for refreshments, two nearby pubs, the Three Horseshoes and The Feathers.*

The main path continues along a road, then over grass along the riverside past Laleham Park, an extensive open space. At its end the path becomes very narrow between the road and the river and you can hear the thunder of traffic from the M3 motorway bridge ahead. Beyond it is Chertsey Lock, from where the path continues on a road to Chertsey Bridge.

🚣 🚌☕🔲 *Chertsey 7 town centre is reached by crossing Chertsey Bridge.*

The Thames Path continues under the bridge, then through a large kissing-gate **F** to follow the river bank through Dumsey Meadow.

As Chertsey Meads open up on the further bank, you have the traditional Thames watermeadow scenes around you for the last time. Where the meadow ends, another kissing-gate leads to a broad, grass path by a number of moored boats. This is the colourful riverside community of Rye Peck Meadow Moorings.

Join a riverside road and walk, wherever possible, along grass strips by the water's edge. You may notice that the bungalows across the river depend on boat links to this bank, as indicated by landing stages, postboxes and even the occasional bell to signal 'Please come and collect me.'

Pass in front of ⬚ the Thames Court and soon, across the Thames, you will see Shepperton Weir, with the spire of Weybridge Church just visible beyond. Then comes Shepperton Lock, with a ☕ café (seasonal opening times) on the island, reached over the lock gates. At the bottom of Ferry Lane just beyond, the path uses one of the few remaining Thames ferries to take you to the Weybridge bank.

≷ ⬚☕ *For Shepperton station, go up Ferry Lane, turn right at the top and follow the road for ½ mile (800 metres). At the war memorial roundabout, carry on up the High Street; at the traffic lights the station is just to your right.*

Contours are given in metres
The vertical interval is 5m

Public transport
Datchet (on route) ≷ 🚌
Staines (0.3 mile/0.5 km) ≷ 🚆 🚌
Chertsey (1.2 miles/2 km) ≷ 🚌
Shepperton (1 mile/1.6 km) ≷ 🚌

Refreshments and toilets
Datchet (on route) ⬚ Royal Stag
Old Windsor (0.2 mile/0.3 km) ⬚ Bells of Ouzeley
Runnymede (on route) ☕ Magna Carta Tea Room, Runnymede Pleasure Grounds Café
Egham (0.7 mile/1.1 km) ⬚ The Crown, The Foresters
Staines (on route) ⬚☕ wide selection
Laleham (on route) ⬚ Three Horseshoes, The Feathers
Chertsey Bridge (on route) ⬚ The Kingfisher; wide selection in town centre
Shepperton Lock (on route) ☕ Shepperton Lock Café (seasonal opening times), ⬚ Thames Court
Shepperton (1mile/1.6 km) ⬚☕ wide selection
Food shops: Windsor, Datchet, Egham, Staines, Chertsey, Shepperton
Public toilets: Windsor, Romney Lock, Old Windsor Lock, Runnymede Pleasure Grounds, Staines, Penton Hook Lock, Laleham Park, Shepperton Lock

Accommodation
Datchet (on route) Lowlands Guest House, Manor Hotel
Old Windsor (0.2 mile/0.3 km) Union Inn, Beaumont House,
Egham (0.7 mile/1.1 km) The Runnymede on Thames, Beau Villa
Staines (on route) wide selection – contact Visitor Information Centre
Laleham (on route) Laleham Park campsite
Chertsey (on route) Crown Hotel, Coach and Horses, Chertsey Caravan and Campsite
Shepperton (0.8 mile/1.3 km) Forty Winks, Splash Cottage, Anchor Hotel, Warren Lodge, Harrisons Hotel

This is the last section of the Thames Path country walk, which finishes at Hampton Court with all the majestic grandeur of Hampton Court Palace as a fitting climax.

The route starts excitingly with a rare ferry crossing, taking you across from Shepperton to the Weybridge bank. If for some reason the ferry is unavailable, an alternative route is signed and described in the text. The towpath here can be busy with cyclists, as the route coincides with National Cycle Network Route 4, here called the Thames Valley Path. After Walton Bridge and Sunbury Lock, the path squeezes past the huge Molesey Reservoirs before opening out through Hampton following an interesting sequence of islands. The Thames Path continues ahead towards Central London and the Thames Barrier, while Teddington, where the tidal Thames truly starts, is only 4¾ miles (7.7 km) further on.

Transport options

Both Weybridge from the ferry and Walton-on-Thames a further 1½ miles (2.4 km) have railway stations but they are some distance from the river. Hampton Court station is very close to the finish.

Things to look out for

1 Shepperton to Weybridge Ferry
Apart from a short period between the 1960s and 1980s, there has been a ferry crossing at this point for at least 500 years. The location was featured in H.G. Wells's famous book *The War of the Worlds*.

2 Walton-on-Thames Close to the Walton Bridge, Walton-on-Thames is a small Surrey town with a long history. It has been suggested that Julius Caesar forded the River Thames here on his second invasion of Britain in 54 BC, but there is no evidence to support this. The parish church of St Mary dates from the 12th century. During the First World War a hospital was set up here at Mount Felix to treat the wounded troops from New Zealand. Memorial services commemorate the links between the two countries.

3 Sunbury Church The distinctive cupola and tower of St Mary's Church in Sunbury is clearly visible across the river on the old Middlesex bank. On the possible site of an early Saxon church, the current building dates from 1752, with recent additions as late as 1972. Charles Dickens knew Sunbury Church and refers to it in *Oliver Twist*.

4 Molesey Reservoirs Behind a long wall along the Surrey side of the river lie the vast Molesey Reservoirs. They were established in the 1870s to serve South West London. Taken out of service in the 1990s, they were then used for aggregate extraction and eventually will be transformed into a wetland area.

5 Sunbury Court This fine mansion dates from 1770. Today it has been converted into an international conference and youth centre.

6 Hampton and Hampton Church Across the river from Hurst Park, the tower of St Mary's Church, Hampton, is framed by trees. Although founded in 1342, the church was completely rebuilt in the early 19th century.

Hampton itself is now part of a London suburb and has been transferred administratively from Middlesex to Surrey. A cannon here marks the place where the first triangulation of the country by the Ordnance Survey was carried out in 1784. Hampton was also the home for a while of the great code-breaker of the Second World War and computer pioneer, Alan Turing.

7 Garrick's Temple to Shakespeare Located on the river bank near Hampton, this little domed temple was built in 1756 by the famous actor-manager David Garrick as a celebration of the life of William Shakespeare. The temple is open to the public on Sunday afternoons between April and October.

8 Hampton Court This magnificent royal palace has an illustrious history. In 1514 Cardinal Thomas Wolsey transformed his private estate by building a vast bishop's palace. He later gave it to Henry VIII, who turned it into the most magnificent palace in the country. In the reign of William and Mary it was redesigned by Sir Christopher Wren and partly rebuilt in the baroque style. Hampton Court Palace and its 60 acres of stunning gardens are open to the public.

Henry VIII's Great Hall at Hampton Court Palace, with its magnificent carved hammerbeam roof.

Route description

From Shepperton Lock you have two options. The old towpath used to cross to the Weybridge bank via the **Shepperton to Weybridge ferry** 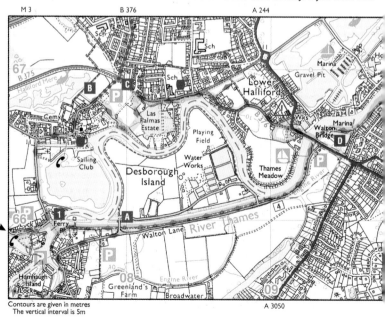 just downstream, and this is the one point on the Thames Path where you can do as the barge teams did – cross by a ferry that still operates. When the ferry is not running, the Thames Path takes an alternative route on the north bank to rejoin the towpath at Walton Bridge.

The Shepperton to Weybridge ferry route

The Shepperton to Weybridge ferry can be summoned by ringing the bell on either bank on the quarter hour. It costs £2 for one journey and runs from 9am to 6pm every day. To confirm any details of the service, please ring the ferry office on 01932 254844.

To visit Weybridge, turn right off the ferry, follow the towpath upstream to Thames Street and keep ahead to reach the High Street. The railway station is beyond the town centre along Monument Hill and Hanger Hill.

Having stepped off the ferry on to the south bank, turn downstream and follow the broad, surfaced track, which soon passes a private footbridge over to an island with a chalet-like house, usually known as D'Oyly Carte Island (see Islands, page 22). Now the old Thames channel can be seen looping away to the left, while the Thames Path goes under a road bridge and straight on beside the Desborough Cut.

The Cut, only completed in 1935, was dug in order to improve the flow of the river, and was named after Lord Desborough, longest-serving chairman of the Thames Conservancy. If you have time

Contours are given in metres
The vertical interval is 5m

to spare, the towpath walk around the old loops of the river is far more rural, if a bit longer. To do this, just take the steps up on the right to cross the road bridge **A**, then carry on by the river to rejoin the Thames Path after crossing the bridge at the far end of the Cut. Beyond the Cut, approaching Walton Bridge, the riverside widens to a popular grass strip where a refreshment hut is often open. Keep ahead to pass beneath Walton Bridge.

≋ ⛉ ⬚ ☕ *To visit Walton-on-Thames* **2**, *turn right beyond the bridge and go up the steps to the main road. Turn left towards the town centre. The railway station is beyond the town centre down Ashley Road and Ashley Park Road.*

The alternative route

To follow this option, walk to the ferry point and turn left away from the river, up Ferry Lane. Turn right at the top to follow the main road past the little Church Square of riverside Shepperton. Turn right again after another 400 yards to cross a car park area **B** on the edge of the public gardens. Walk on through a gap into Manor Park with a brick wall to your right, keeping by the wall on the enclosed path until it ends, and you can bear right to the riverside. This idyllic spot is one of the Shepperton Loops, no longer the main channel but still navigable. Turn left along the riverside, but look back for a delightful view of the Manor House and its lawns by the river.

This is but the briefest of encounters with the river, so after 130 yards (120 metres) bear left into the trees and shortly turn sharp left across an open grass area. Walk over a wooden plank bridge and then along a path with a cricket field on your left, which soon brings you to another small car park. Bear right across this for a few yards before turning right again on to

a winding path through trees. Soon you go right over a wooden footbridge towards the road, turning right again to follow the path parallel to it. Emerge from the trees and eventually join the busy A375 **C**.

Keep ahead and as soon as you come to an area of open grass, take the gravel path which heads diagonally right towards a big, white, weatherboarded cottage. At the end of this path, where you come out on a road, turn right and continue along Walton Lane until you eventually come to a busy road junction. Here you should use the pedestrian islands to reach the far pavement and follow it to the right to cross Walton Bridge. On the south side, take the steps on the left leading down to a path that doubles back to join the towpath **D**.

≋ ⛉ ⬚ ☕ *Keep ahead across the bridge to visit Walton-on-Thames* **2** *town centre.*

Walton Bridge is a bland-looking bridge but with a fascinating history (see Bridges, page 19). It is going to be replaced with a new single-span bridge between January 2012 and summer 2013. The old bridge will remain open during the works and any changes to the route kept to a minimum. Please follow the signs at all times.

Beyond Walton Bridge, the broad track soon continues, over a marina entry on a large footbridge and past a couple of riverside pubs, ⬚ The Swan and The Anglers, which form part of the old Walton Wharf. Pass the Thames Valley Skiff Club and a community of small houses on the opposite bank. Beyond St George's Boat Club comes the big, factory-like block of Elmbridge Leisure Centre, which has a useful ☕ public cafeteria. Ahead now is Sunbury Weir

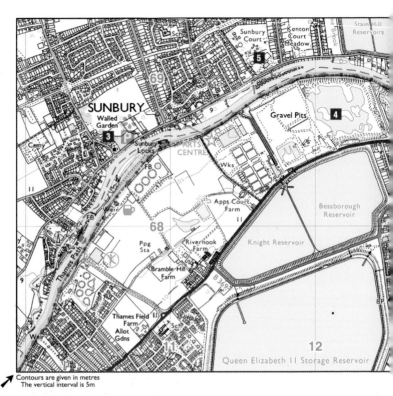

Contours are given in metres
The vertical interval is 5m

and, visible beyond it, the tower and cupola of **Sunbury Church** ❸. Close to the 🍴 Weir Hotel, you negotiate two gates and a bike-free section of path, before reaching the original lock house, with 1812 inscribed on its facia tablet. The original lock stood here, but today's Sunbury Locks, two of them side by side, are further downstream.

Along the next stretch, the path is overshadowed by the walls and banks of the **Molesey Reservoirs** ❹, a claustrophobic walk. Some way along, you will glimpse a fine house across the river: **Sunbury Court** ❺, partly hidden by the bungalows on the island in front. Hereabouts, too, you will walk between great concrete blocks, remains of London's anti-tank defences. When the

reservoirs end, you will find yourself walking along a gradually widening grass strip – once part of Hurst Park Racecourse.

Across the river are the houses of riverside **Hampton** and the narrow tower of **Hampton Church** ❻. Beyond Garrick Ait and looking back, you will see the domed **Garrick temple** ❼. On our own bank, the proclaimed 'swan feeding area' is clearly successful, attracting a wide range of waterfowl and pigeons.

Several more islands follow, the longest hosting an impressive array of palatial houseboats. Continue now to Molesey Lock, which has public toilets to the right. Just beyond it there is a gravel path near the riverside, which curves up to the road just before Hampton Court Bridge.

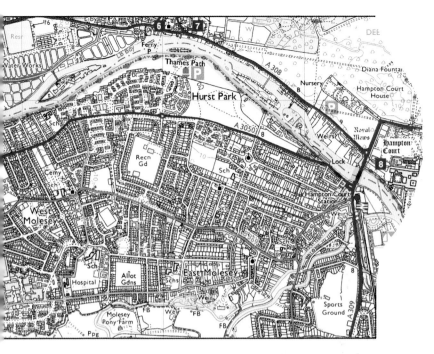

≋ *Hampton Court station is across the road to your right here.*

Congratulations – you have now reached the end of the Thames Path as covered by this National Trail Guide. The majestic regal splendour of Hampton Court Palace **8** makes a dramatic finish to a wonderful walk. This is not the end of the National Trail, however: the remaining 38 miles (61 km) of the Thames Path run on through the centre of London to the Thames Barrier and are described in the companion volume, *Thames Path in London*, published by Aurum Press.

Public transport

Weybridge (1.2 mile/ 1.9 km) ≋ 🚌
Walton-on-Thames (1 mile/ 1.6 km) ≋ 🚌
Hampton Court (on route) ≋ 🚌

Refreshments and toilets

Walton-on-Thames (on route) ☕ George Inn, The Swan, The Anglers; ☕ Elmbridge Xcel Leisure Centre Caféteria
Sunbury Lock (on route) ☕ Weir Hotel
Hampton Court (on route) ☕ Kings Arms
Food shops: Shepperton, Weybridge, Walton-on-Thames

Public toilets: Shepperton Lock, Walton Bridge, Sunbury Lock, Molesey Lock

Accommodation

Weybridge (1.2 mile/ 1.9 km) wide selection – contact Kingston Visitor Information Centre
Walton-on-Thames (on route) George Inn, The Cottage
Sunbury Lock (on route) Weir Hotel
Hampton Court (on route) Kings Arms, Lion Gate Hotel, Carlton Mitre
Hampton (1.2 miles/ 1.9 km) The Chestnuts

Useful Information

Contact details

This section includes details of telephone numbers, websites and email addresses where available. If no email address is shown, it may be possible to send an email via the website.

Thames Path National Trail Office

Signal Court, Old Station Way, Eynsham, Oxfordshire OX29 4TL

(i) www.nationaltrail.co.uk/thamespath
✉ nationaltrails@oxfordshire.gov.uk
☎ 01865 810224

National Trails Office

Block B, Government Buildings, Whittington Road, Worcester WR5 2LQ

(i) www.nationaltrail.co.uk
✉ national.trail@naturalengland.org.uk

Environment Agency
(responsible for the River Thames)

(i) www.environment-agency.gov.uk
☎ 0370 850 6506

Environment Agency
Flood Information Line

☎ 0845 988 1188

Travel information

National Rail Enquiries

(i) www.nationalrail.co.uk
☎ 0845 748 4950 (Traintracker automated service on 0871 200 4950)

Traveline

(i) www.traveline.org.uk
☎ 0871 200 2233

London Transport (bus, underground, overground, Docklands Light Railway, boat)

(i) www.tfl.gov.uk
☎ 0843 222 1234

First Great Western

(i) www.firstgreatwestern.co.uk
☎ 0845 700 0125

South West Trains

(i) www.southwesttrains.co.uk
☎ 0845 600 0650

National Express Coaches

(i) www.nationalexpress.com/coach
☎ 08717 818178

Oxford Tube (London–Oxford buses)

(i) www.oxfordtube.com
☎ 01865 772250

Oxford Bus Company (express and local services)

(i) www.oxfordbus.co.uk
✉ info@oxfordbus.co.uk
☎ 01865 785400

Boat services outside London

Salters Steamers

(i) www.salterssteamers.co.uk
✉ info@salterssteamers.co.uk
☎ 01865 243421

Accommodation

The Thames Path Companion, an up-to-date and comprehensive guide to facilities and accommodation along the length of the Thames Path, is available at £4.95 from the National Trails Office, Signal Court, Old Station Way, Eynsham, Oxfordshire OX29 4TL;
☎ 01865 810224;
✉ nationaltrails@oxfordshire.gov.uk

Tourist information

Visit Britain

(i) www.visitbritain.com

Tourism South East

(i) www.visitsoutheastengland.com

Cirencester Visitor Information Centre

(i) www.cirencester.gov.uk
☎ 01285 654180

Swindon Visitor Information Centre

(i) www.visitwiltshire.co.uk
☎ 01793 466454

Faringdon Visitor Information Centre

(i) www.faringdon.org/tttourism1.htm
☎ 01367 242191

Witney Visitor Information Centre
(i) www.oxfordshirecotswolds.org
☎ 01993 775802

Oxford Visitor Information Centre
(i) www.visitoxfordandoxfordshire.com
☎ 01865 252200

Abingdon Visitor Information Centre
(i) www.abingdon.gov.uk
☎ 01235 522711

Wallingford Visitor Information Centre
(i) www.visitsouthoxfordshire.co.uk
01491 826972

Reading Visitor Information Centre
(i) www.livingreading.co.uk
☎ 0118 900 1624

Henley-on-Thames Visitor Information Centre
(i) www.visitsouthoxfordshire.co.uk
☎ 01491 578034

Kingston-on-Thames Visitor Information Centre
(i) www.kingstonfirst.co.uk
☎ 0208 546 1140

London Visitor Information Centre
(i) www.visitlondon.com
☎ 0870 156 6366

Marlow Visitor Information Centre
(i) www.visitbuckinghamshire.org
☎ 01628 483597

Maidenhead Visitor Information Centre
(i) www.windsor.gov.uk
☎ 01628 796502

Windsor Visitor Information Centre
(i) www.windsor.gov.uk
☎ 01753 743907

County, borough and district councils

Buckinghamshire County Council
(i) www.buckscc.gov.uk
☎ 0845 230 2882

Gloucestershire County Council
(i) www.gloucestershire.gov.uk
☎ 01452 425577

Oxfordshire County Council
(i) www.oxfordshire.gov.uk
☎ 01865 810226

Reading Borough Council
(i) www.reading.gov.uk
☎ 0800 626540

Royal Borough of Windsor and Maidenhead
(i) www.rbwm.gov.uk
☎ 01628 683800

Surrey County Council
(i) www.surreycc.gov.uk/countryside
☎ 0345 600 9009

Swindon Borough Council
(i) www.swindon.gov.uk
☎ 01793 445500

West Berkshire Council
(i) www.westberks.gov.uk
☎ 01635 42400

Wiltshire County Council
(i) www.wiltshire.gov.uk
☎ 01225 756178

Wokingham District Council
(i) www.wokingham.gov.uk
☎ 0118 974 6000

Other contacts

Berkshire, Buckinghamshire and Oxford Wildlife Trust
(i) www.bbowt.org.uk
✎ info@bbowt.org.uk
☎ 01865 775476

Chilterns Area of Outstanding Natural Beauty
(i) www.chilternsaonb.org
✎ info@chilternsaonb.org.uk
☎ 01844 355500

Churches Conservation Trust
(i) www.visitchurches.org.uk
✎ central@tcct.org.uk
☎ 0207 213 0660

Cotswold Canals Trust (Thames–Severn Canal)
ⓘ www.cotswoldcanals.com
✉ mail@cotswoldcanals.com
☎ 01453 752568

Cotswold Water Park
ⓘ www.waterpark.org
✉ info@waterpark.org
☎ 01793 752413

Earth Trust Environmental Charity
(formerly Northmoor Trust)
ⓘ www.earthtrust.org.uk
✉ admin@earthtrust.org.uk
☎ 01865 407792

English Heritage
ⓘ www.english-heritage.org.uk
✉ customers@english-heritage.org.uk
☎ 0870 333 1181

Gloucestershire Wildlife Trust
ⓘ www.gloucestershirewildlifetrust.org.uk
✉ info@gloucestershirewildlifetrust.org.uk
☎ 01452 383333

Kennet and Avon Canal Trust
ⓘ www.katrust.co.uk
☎ 01380 721279

Long Distance Walkers Association
ⓘ www.ldwa.org.uk
✉ secretary@ldwa.org.uk

National Trust
ⓘ www.nationaltrust.org.uk
✉ enquiries@nationaltrust.org.uk
☎ 0844 800 1895

North Wessex Downs AONB
ⓘ www.northwessexdowns.org.uk
✉ info@northwessexdowns.org.uk
☎ 01488 685440

Open Spaces Society
ⓘ www.oss.org.uk
☎ 01491 573535

Ordnance Survey
ⓘ www.ordnancesurvey.co.uk
✉ customerservices@ordnancesurvey.co.uk
☎ 0845 605 0505

Ramblers Association
ⓘ www.ramblers.org.uk
✉ ramblers@ramblers.org.uk
☎ 0207 339 8500

River and Rowing Museum, Henley
ⓘ www.rrm.co.uk
✉ museum@rrm.co.uk
☎ 01491 415600

River Thames Society
ⓘ www.riverthamessociety.org.uk
✉ admin@riverthamessociety.org.uk
☎ 01491 612456

RSPB
ⓘ www.rspb.org.uk
☎ 01767 680551

Society of Antiquaries (Kelmscott Manor)
ⓘ www.sal.org.uk
✉ admin@sal.org.uk
☎ 0207 479 7080

Stanley Spencer Gallery
ⓘ www.stanleyspencer.org.uk
☎ 01628 471885

Surrey Wildlife Trust
ⓘ www.surreywildlifetrust.org.uk
✉ info@surreywt.org.uk
☎ 01483 795440

Sustrans
ⓘ www.sustrans.org.uk
✉ info@sustrans.org.uk
☎ 0845 113 0065

Thames Heritage Trust
ⓘ www.thamesheritage.org.uk
✉ info@thamesheritage.org.uk
☎ 01420 86888

Thames Rivers Restoration Trust
ⓘ www.trrt.org.uk

Wiltshire Wildlife Trust
ⓘ www.wiltshirewildlife.org
✉ info@wiltshirewildlife.org
☎ 01380 725670

Woodland Trust
ⓘ www.woodlandtrust.org.uk
✉ enquiries@woodlandtrust.org.uk
☎ 01476 581135

Youth Hostel association
ⓘ www.yha.org.uk
✉ customerservices@yha.org.uk
☎ 0800 019 1700

Useful contacts for Oxford circular walk

Christchurch College Cathedral and Meadow
(i) www.chch.ox.ac.uk
☎ 01865 276492

Merton College
(i) www.merton.ox.ac.uk
☎ 01865 276310

Bodleian Library
(i) www.bodleian.ox.ac.uk
☎ 01865 277224

Magdalen College
(i) www.magd.ox.ac.uk
☎ 01865 276000

Oxford Botanic Garden
(i) www.botanic-garden.ox.ac.uk
☎ 01865 286690

Oxford University Parks
(i) www.parks.ox.ac.uk/closing/index.htm
☎ 01865 282040

Oxford Castle
(i) www.oxfordcastle.com
☎ 01865 260666

Useful contacts for Windsor and Eton circular walk

Eton College
(i) www.etoncollege.com/publicvisits.aspx
☎ 01753 671177 (Visits Manager)

Windsor Castle
(i) www.royalcollection.org.uk .
☎ 0207 766 7304

Further reading

A brief selection of the more interesting titles about the River Thames. Those out of print may be available through public libraries or online booksellers.

Ackroyd, Peter, *Thames: Sacred River* (Vintage, 2006).
Batey, Mavis, Buttery, Henrietta, Lambert, David, and Wilkie, Kim, *Arcadian Thames* (Barn Elms, 1994).
Bolland, R. S., *Victorians on the Thames* (Midas Books, 1974).
Brabbs, Derry, *The River Thames* (Frances Lincoln, 2010).
Cove-Smith, Chris, *River Thames Book* (Imray, 2009).
Goldsack, Paul, *River Thames: In the Footsteps of the Famous* (Bradt, 2002).
Mackay, Duncan, *The Secret Thames* (Ebury Press/Countryside Commission, 1992).
Phillips, Geoffrey, *Thames Crossings* (David & Charles, 1981).
Schneer, Jonathan, *The Thames: England's River* (Abacus, 2006).
Winn Christopher, *I never knew that about the River Thames* (Ebury Press, 2010).

Ordnance Survey maps covering the Thames Path in the Country

Landranger Maps (scale 1:50 000): 163, 164, 174, 175, 176
Explorer Maps (scale 1:25 000): 168 Stroud, Tetbury and Malmesbury; 169 Cirencester and Swindon; 170 Abingdon, Wantage and Vale of White Horse; 180 Oxford; 171 Chiltern Hills West; 172 Chiltern Hills East; 160 Windsor, Weybridge and Bracknell; 161 London South

The Official Guides to all o

Cotswold Way
Anthony Burton

100 miles of quintessentially
English landscape

ISBN 978 1 84513 785 4

Cleveland Way
Ian Sampson

Over 100 miles of magnificent
walking on the North York Moors

ISBN 978 1 84513 781 6

Pennine Way
Damian Hall

The whole of England's toughest
National Trail

ISBN 978 1 84513 718 2

Yorkshire Wolds Way
Roger Ratcliffe

A superbly tranquil walk through the
unspoilt chalk hills of East Yorkshire

ISBN 978 1 84513 643 7

Pembrokeshire Coast Path
Brian John

180 miles of clifftop, beach and cove
around the magnificent Welsh coast

ISBN 978 1 84513 602 4

South Downs Way
Paul Millmore

100 miles of glorious chalk downland
for the walker, cyclist and horse rider

ISBN 978 1 84513 565 2

Hadrian's Wall Path
Anthony Burton

Follow the Roman Wall
from coast to coast

ISBN 978 1 84513 567 6

The Ridgeway
Anthony Burton

87 miles of downland walking
from Wiltshire to the Chilterns

ISBN 978 1 84513 638 3

North Downs Way
Colin Saunders

Follow the chalk ridge across South-East
England all the way to the sea

ISBN 978 1 84513 677 2